WHA

If you've forgotten that God h   w provides the course correction yo   efreshingly into the heart, *Meant for Good* reveals   s under God's grace and in the center of His faithful plan. … This soul-replenishing Bible study reveals that, even through trial and suffering, your precious life as God's child is meant for good.

Michael W. Newman, President of the Texas District LCMS and author
of Hope When Your Heart Breaks and Getting Through Grief

This study is a beautiful reminder that trusting God beyond what we can see is key to walking in His will. Donna carefully crafts each chapter, fills it with insightful commentary and history, and provides questions that will lead you deeper into scripture and help you apply it to your life.

Michelle Diercks, speaker and author of *Promised Rest: Finding Peace in God's Presence*

Understanding God's purposes and plans is difficult for anyone, and Joseph was no exception. Donna directs us to God's call to walk in blind trust regardless of the outcome, showing how God's plan of salvation is clearly foreshadowed in Joseph, a suffering servant and a picture of Jesus.

Rev. Dr. Greg Walton, VP, Ministry Solutions – Grace Place Wellness,
Lutheran Church Extension Fund

We might think we know everything about this Old Testament character from Sunday School lessons and Broadway musicals, but author Donna Snow masterfully uncovers themes of spiritual maturity, forgiveness, reconciliation, family dynamics, and God's providential will. As you revisit the story of Joseph, you will see that while God's work in our lives may seem like a confusing puzzle, it's always meant for good.

Sharla Fritz, author of several CPH books, including *Measured by Grace: How God Defines Success*

Without shying away or ignoring hard biblical truths, Donna Snow paints the story of Joseph and his family into vivid color, relevance, and practical application for women looking to trust God in difficult circumstances and amidst myriad challenges. This is the perfect study for participants who desire in-depth study steeped richly in God's Word.

Jessica R. Patch, *Publisher's Weekly* bestselling author

Most of us are familiar with the Old Testament tale of Joseph and those meddlesome brothers of his. Joseph was a dreamer, but his were God's dreams. Donna Snow's new study, *Meant for Good,* is a deep dive into Joseph's journey from prisoner to prosperity and power that gives keen insight into God's plan for us in our own times of adversity. I found touchpoint in this study that I have incorporated into my own life, and I believe you will too.

Kathleen Y'Barbo Turner, *Publishers Weekly* Bestselling Author
of Dog Days of Summer and The Bark of Zorro

Meant for Good is meant for you! Donna nails it again with her comprehensive study that unpacks the history and political play of the day, all while keeping you hooked until the last page with biblical, practical, thought-provoking, and meaningful application. Despite apparent loss and defeat, Joseph is a story of perseverance and God's goodness. This study spoke to my life—struggles, difficulties, and questions—how God meant them for good. Clear references to Christ assure us of God's guaranteed grace and that, in Jesus, we definitely have enough. Don't wait. Dig in today!

Rev. Andrew Ratcliffe, Pastor at St. Paul's Lutheran Church and School

Donna Snow's enthusiasm for God's Word is contagious, and I couldn't wait to see Joseph through her eyes. And boy, she didn't disappoint! Layered with spiritual depth, and cultural and historical context, this book meets me in my everyday experience. Donna's words will weave around you like a multicolored tapestry, rich with the mystery and miracle of Joseph's story that reveals the heart of God.

Lindsay Hausch, Author of Take Heart: God's Comfort for Anxious Thoughts
and God's Provision in a Wilderness World

With honest and inviting personal reflections, Donna Snow draws us into an in-depth look at the life of Joseph. Her " Go Quiet and Go Deep" process and Scripture scribing opportunities allow personal reflection space with an Old Testament story that speaks right into our modern family drama settings. Difficult challenges today can add to spiritual dehydration, but this study offers grace and peace with volumes of hope for each of our faith journeys.

Connie Denninger, Co-Founder of Visual Faith® Ministry

Donna Snow is an excellent and prolific author who equips Bible students to grow in their knowledge of God's Word. In her newest Bible study, she helps us recognize issues and challenges that Joseph and Jesus faced. She digs deep, includes research about religious customs and beliefs, and equips us to apply God's Word to our daily life. I highly recommend this book.

Kay L. Meyer, Founder, President and Host, Family Shield Ministries, Inc

I became a big fan of Donna Snow after reading *Chosen,* her book on Esther. Her study of Joseph is equally impactful. Donna's writing is accessible and personal and has great depth. Her newest book feels like a friend guiding you through the story of Joseph. Extensive research is evident. Along with engaging the mind, the book also reaches the heart by bringing encouragement and hope from God's Word. Throughout *Meant for Good,* Donna keeps Christ at the center, showing us how Joseph's story—and our story—intersect with our Savior's story.

Rev. Dr. Christopher Kennedy, Senior Pastor at Shepherd
of the Hills Lutheran Church, School, and Child Care

MEANT
FOR
GOOD

A STUDY OF JOSEPH

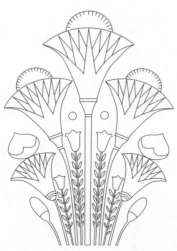

DONNA SNOW

CONCORDIA PUBLISHING HOUSE · SAINT LOUIS

Published by Concordia Publishing House
3558 S. Jefferson Ave., St. Louis, MO 63118-3968
1-800-325-3040 • cph.org

1   2   3   4   5   6   7   8   9   10   32   31   30   29   28   27   26   25   24   23

DEDICATION

This book is dedicated to you because it used to be me.
We were lost, but now we are found.
Because of Jesus.

His love and sacrifice reconcile us back to God.
His shoulders carry our differences, weaknesses, and brokenness.
Now we are empowered with this ministry of reconciliation.
Because of Jesus.

Our world desperately needs His love and grace.
What are we waiting for? The time is now.
Let's get out there and make some peace.
Because of Jesus.

CONTENTS

An Introduction
to Our Study of Joseph

Of all his children, Jacob loved Joseph best. Though Jacob had ten older sons, Joseph was the firstborn of the wife Jacob loved above all. Joseph was a bright, handsome child and was his father's pet—just as Jacob had once been his mother's pet (family patterns often repeat).

The story begins with Joseph as a seventeen-year-old dreamer—literally. God gave Joseph the gift of interpreting dreams—but he had not yet mastered the art of tact, timing, or knowing his audience. When he tells his brothers that one day they will bow to him, it becomes clear that even though Joseph's gift was intact, he was not able to read a room.

One day, Jacob sends Joseph to check on his brothers, who are tending the flock far away. But Joseph never makes it back home to deliver his report to Jacob. The brothers accost Joseph, strip him of his many-colored coat, and throw him into a waterless pit. Even though Joseph's brothers stripped him of his coat, they could not strip him of his character.

They sell Joseph to Midianite traders (also sometimes referred to as Ishmaelites) for a profit and go about their day. So begins Joseph's spiritual boot camp, which lasts more than twenty years. The amazing truth about God's spiritual boot camps (basically, our whole life) is that He never leaves us. Ever.

During those twenty years, Joseph oversees Potiphar's home, is unjustly thrown into prison, and interprets four dreams for other people. God is working in Joseph's life. Molding. Shaping. Preparing. Finally, God elevates Joseph to second-in-command over all the land. Only then does God orchestrate a family reunion between Joseph and his family.

We behold the Gospel story woven like a scarlet thread throughout Joseph's narrative. The struggles that Joseph endures remind us how vital it is to let God's love and forgiveness lead us. This is not a rags-to-riches phenomenon.

In Joseph, we see Christlike qualities and parallels to apply to our Christian walk. We can choose to become victims of our circumstances, or we can trust God to bring beauty from ashes every single time.

Joseph's biography occupies more space in Genesis than those of Adam, Noah, Abraham, or even Joseph's own father, Jacob. Even though that should be reason enough to study Joseph's incredible journey, he also experiences family conflict and unfair treatment, which many of us can relate to today.

When God shows us that He will use us, we usually want to dive right in. In reality, it may be a long time before God deems us ready for the tasks He has planned for us. Joseph, rather than becoming bitter, responded to broken dreams and impossible circumstances with a faith that propelled him from the pit of slavery to the pinnacle of power.

Perhaps you and I can relate to waterless pits and unfairness in our lives. By the end of the story, God uses Joseph to provide invaluable insights regarding how to live out wise, bold journeys of faith in our everyday Christian walk.

TIMELINE, JOSEPH'S LINEAGE, EGYPT'S PHARAOHS, AND ANCIENT EGYPT

DATE	EVENT(S)
1901–1897 BC	Joseph is sold into slavery in Egypt (Genesis 37:2, 12–28)
1888–1884 BC	Joseph enters into service in Pharaoh's court (Genesis 41:46)
1876 BC	Jacob goes to Egypt (Genesis 47:9, 28; Exodus 12:40–41)
1859 BC	Jacob dies (Genesis 49:33)
1808–1804 BC	Joseph dies (Genesis 50:22, 26)

Joseph's Lineage

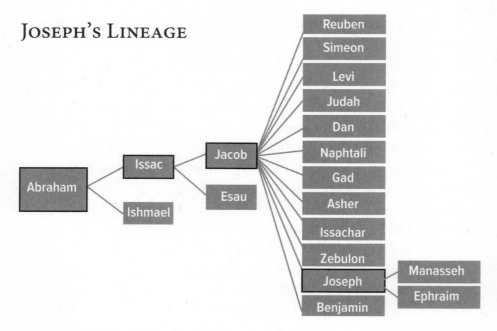

Jacob's twelve sons, with the exception of Joseph, comprised the twelve tribes of Israel. Joseph's two sons, Manasseh and Ephraim, each counted as a half-tribe to make the twelfth tribe together. There is no tribe named Joseph. Our Lord and Savior Jesus Christ's earthly lineage came through the tribe of Judah.

Egypt's Pharaohs

Although Egypt's early rulers were referred to as kings, eventually, they became known as pharaohs based on where they lived. The word *pharaoh* means "great house." An Egyptian pharaoh served as the primary overseer and ruler over all the land.

Along with being the ruler over Egypt, a pharaoh was viewed as the religious leader of the people. Egyptians believed pharaohs to be divine intermediaries between their Egyptian gods and themselves. Archaeologists have discovered that, among other tasks, pharaohs participated in religious ceremonies, created and imposed laws, declared war, levied taxes, and generally had control over everything throughout Egypt.

It may be interesting to note that pharaohs were not always men. Historians have revealed that Cleopatra was, in fact, a pharaoh. Another noteworthy and successful female pharaoh was Hatshepsut. In the fifteenth century BC, Hatshepsut's stunning temple, called the Deir el-Bahri, was built into the cliffs along the Nile River near the entrance of the Valley of the Kings. It still stands today and is an impressive structure to visit and explore.

However, many inscriptions and monuments that mentioned her were destroyed after Hatshepsut's death. Scholars believe that this may have been to prevent women from becoming pharaohs in future generations. Other scholars, however, have suggested that Hatsheput was the daughter who rescued Moses, and the destruction of these tributes to her was retaliation for her having brought the man who would eventually cause the destruction of Egypt through the plagues into Pharaoh's home.[1]

Joseph lived during the historical period known as the Middle Kingdom, which lasted roughly 2000–1786 BCE. This is considered one of Egypt's greatest eras. Joseph most likely began serving under Sesostris III (1878–1841 BC). Joseph lived in Egypt for seventy-one years and died in approximately 1805 BC, under the reign of Amenemhet III (1841–1797 BCE).[2]

Sesostris III was the fifth of eight ancient Egyptian kings who reigned during Egypt's Twelfth Dynasty.[3] He was instrumental in reshaping the government of Egypt and even extended Egypt's holdings into Nubia, just to the south.

During Sesostris III's reign, he created powerful government departments that were put under the watch of his vizier (or prime minister). These included departments of treasury, agriculture, war, and labor. The vizier kept strict accounts of the kingdom's income and expenses, which remained standard practice over the next one hundred years. This is likely the role Joseph held, though it cannot be absolutely confirmed through historical records.

The pharaoh Joseph served under granted permission for Joseph to move his entire family to Goshen, the lushest and most fertile land in all of Egypt. However, after Joseph's death (where our study ends), "there arose a new king over Egypt, who did not know Joseph" (Exodus 1:8). And by God's design, Israel endured harsh slavery during the last decades of their four hundred years in Egypt.

Then, in God's perfect timing, God liberated His people from Egypt in arguably the most dramatic display of His power and glory in all of Scripture, apart from the resurrection.

ANCIENT EGYPT

Originally starting out as several independent cities along the Nile River, Egypt was formed from an Upper Egypt and Lower Egypt, which unified around 3100 BC. Egypt was one the largest kingdoms of the ancient world and led the charge regarding cultural and economic influence until it was conquered in 332 BC by the Macedonians.

HELPFUL INSIGHTS FOR OUR STUDY

CHARACTER STUDY

Joseph is an extraordinary patriarch in Scripture. We see the divine plan of God unfolding through the patriarchs. In Abraham, we see the power of God. In Isaac, we see the provision of God. In Jacob, we see the purpose of God. And in Joseph, we see the plan of God.

The Bible faithfully paints the patriarchs and prominent leaders with warts and all. We see their faults, sins, and deceptions. However, we must press our nose against the glass very close to find Joseph's warts. In fact, many interpreters throughout Church history have seen Joseph as one of the most Christlike figures in Scripture.

More detailed biographical information is provided about Joseph than almost any other person in the Old Testament. But more important, through-out Joseph's life, we see the Gospel theme of goodness and God's covenant promise for the faithful.

JOSEPH IS A PORTRAIT OF JESUS

Out of all the Old Testament cast of characters, Joseph offers us a re-markable picture of Jesus. In my opinion, he more closely models Christ than any other. In countless ways, the life of Joseph parallels the future life of Jesus. Specifically, Joseph

- was a shepherd deeply loved by his father;
- was hated and rejected by his brothers;
- was put into a pit and assumed dead but was raised up;
- was sold for pieces of silver and turned over to Gentiles;
- endured severe temptation but did not sin;
- was accused falsely but spoke no defense;
- was cast into prison yet shared a message of deliverance;
- was honored among Gentiles yet rejected by his brothers;
- married a Gentile bride;

- began his life's work at thirty years old;

- became the only source of bread for the world;

- desired that all his brothers come to him;

- created fellowship with his brothers after they repented and knew his identity; and

- provided for his brothers, including a place to live with him.

His brothers also proclaimed his glory after his death.

JOSEPH'S TESTS

Joseph endured great suffering in a pit, in Potiphar's house, and as a prisoner—tests that provided the character-building strength Joseph would need to fulfill what God had planned for his life. (We will dive deeper into these three *P*s as our study moves along.)

Even when Joseph passed the tests and was elevated by the pharaoh, prosperity and power did not ruin him. His character remained consistent in both public and private spaces. His work ethic and commitment are models of Christlike dedication to God. He never complained nor compromised.

As we look at Joseph's life, I pray that we learn from it and pass our tests as well as Joseph did. But more important, I pray that God gives us the grace and strength to model Jesus as well as Joseph's life did.

WEEK 1

THE DREAMER

Genesis 37

In Genesis 37, we are introduced to one of the most detailed, remarkable life stories in the entire Old Testament. Joseph experienced great love, parental favoritism, destructive hatred, enslavement, temptation, imprisonment, exaltation, and power.

Yet throughout his life, Joseph remained moldable by God. His obedience and faithfulness to God are some of the most sterling, Christlike examples in all of Scripture.

DAY 1   Dark Clouds of Favoritism *(Genesis 37:1–4)*

DAY 2   The Meaning of Dreams *(Genesis 37:5–9)*

DAY 3   Journey into the Storm *(Genesis 37:12–17)*

DAY 4   Lightning Rod of Hatred *(Genesis 37:18–24)*

DAY 5   Sold Out *(Genesis 37:25–35)*

KEY QUESTIONS:

- Have you ever experienced favoritism? If so, what was the result?

- Self-centeredness sat at the heart of Joseph's brothers' lives—what sits at the heart of yours?

- Has there been a time in your life when you felt like God had hidden His face from your circumstances, only to realize He was there all along? What did you learn from that experience?

DAY 1

DARK CLOUDS OF FAVORITISM

Now Israel loved Joseph more than any other of his sons, because he was the son of his old age. And he made him a robe of many colors. (Genesis 37:3)

We begin our study in the land of Canaan. Later known as the Promised Land, Canaan was named after one of the sons of Ham (see Genesis 10:6). Ham was one of Noah's three sons, whom God preserved on the ark during the flood. Let's start by grasping some basic history.

In Genesis 17:8, what did God promise to Joseph's great-grandfather Abraham?

Canaan would be an everlasting possession of Abraham and his descendants for all time. As the great-grandson of Abraham, Joseph and his family still lived there.

Modern-day Canaan includes parts of Syria, Lebanon, Jordan, Israel, the Gaza Strip, and the West Bank. Since it has changed rulership many times in history, this particular area of the world is the center of ongoing conflict.

When we pick up the narrative of Joseph's life, he is already a teenager. And his family life certainly does not appear to be all peaches and cream.

Read Genesis 37:1–4. What stands out to you in these verses?

Drama! There is a lot going on in these four verses. One of the first things to jump out is that Joseph has half-siblings: "the sons of Bilhah and Zilpah, his father's wives." If you have ever navigated life with half-siblings, then you know it can certainly be challenging. So who are these two women in relation to Joseph?

JACOB'S SONS

After fleeing home when he stole his brother Esau's blessing, Jacob ended up at the house of his uncle Laban. Jacob agreed to work for his uncle for seven years in exchange for permission to marry Laban's lovely daughter— Rachel. After Laban deceived him by giving him his older daughter—Leah— in place of Rachel, Jacob worked an extra seven years for Rachel's hand (see Genesis 29:1–30). From them (and their handmaidens) were born twelve sons, who would become the twelve tribes of Israel.

Leah bore four sons (see Genesis 29:31–35), but Rachel could not conceive, so she offered to Jacob her handmaiden Bilhah to bear children on her behalf. (This was a common practice in those days to secure family dynasties.) And then the plot thickens even more.

Read Genesis 30:1–24.

Take some time to fill in which women gave birth to which sons in the chart below:

SCRIPTURE	MOTHER	SONS
Genesis 29:31–35	Leah	1. 2. 3. 4. Judah
Genesis 30:1–8	Bilhah (Rachel's handmaiden)	5. Dan 6. naphlele
Genesis 30:9–13	Zilpah (Leah's handmaiden)	7. 8.
Genesis 30:17–20	Leah	9. 10.
Genesis 30:22–24	Rachel	11.
Genesis 35:16–19	Rachel	12.

All in all, Jacob (also called Israel) had eight of his twelve sons with his two wives and four with his wives' two handmaidens. Scholars generally agree that all twelve sons were born within a decade and a half since four different women bore them. Only Jacob's youngest sons, Joseph and Benjamin, shared Rachel as their mother.

According to Genesis 29:30, how did Jacob feel about Rachel?

Here we see the dark clouds of favoritism appear on the horizon. Joseph was the firstborn son of the woman that Jacob loved the most. Benjamin was the youngest, also born to Rachel; she died giving birth to him.

Do you have half-siblings in your family? If so, how has that been a challenge or a blessing?

My dad was married to a lady before my mom and had four children with her. Consequently, I have four older half-siblings through my dad. Only my half-brother, Donnie, and I have any kind of relationship. Though he lives in Kansas, we stay in touch via Facebook and exchanging Christmas cards. My three half-sisters pretty much keep to themselves. I understand firsthand the awkwardness and emotions that come with half-siblings.

When Joseph initially appears in Scripture, he is already seventeen years old. We know next to nothing about his boyhood years except where his father sojourned. This is another place where we see a similarity between Joseph and Jesus.

We know next to nothing of Jesus' boyhood years, except the incident when a twelve-year-old Jesus stayed behind in Jerusalem to talk to the scholars in the temple. When his parents scolded Jesus for worrying them, Jesus responded, "Did you not know that I must be in My Father's house?" (Luke 2:49). Jesus' behavior was not sinful but righteous in that He was obeying His Father. We cannot stretch this analogy too far, but it can be reasonable to assume a likely scenario played out in Joseph's situation.

TATTLETALE OR OBEDIENT SON?
What does Genesis 37:2 tell us?

This story just keeps adding complex layers. Now it appears that Joseph may be a tattletale. At this point, Scripture does not reveal why Joseph was reporting on his brothers, much less why he was giving a bad report about them. But that certainly does not bode well for forming a close familial bond with those brothers. We will look deeper into this subject on Day 3, but it certainly explains the friction between Joseph and the others.

THE DARK CLOUDS OF FAVORITISM
In Genesis 37:3–4, what family issue has surfaced?

Here we see sibling rivalry at its worst (not that there's ever a best). Any parent with more than one child has struggled with sibling rivalry, and playing favorites makes it worse. Sometimes parents do favor one child over another, although they may explain their love as simply "different" rather than "favorite."

If you have siblings, are you considered your parents' favorite child? If so, what difficulties or blessings have resulted?

A family that I was acquainted with years ago allowed a rift to form after the grandmother passed away. The grown children fought over her money and possessions. Ugly words were exchanged, which could not be unsaid, and unforgiveness took hold.

To this day, that family's siblings, now in their eighties, refuse to make amends or communicate. Consequently, their children have grown up never knowing their aunts, uncles, or cousins on that side of the family. The sins of greed and unforgiveness have wrought unnecessary, wasteful destruction. Inheritance rights and allotments can certainly cause issues.

Have you experienced that in your own family, or do you know families that have? If so, were those issues worked through or did they cause long-term hard feelings?

Our society tends to value collecting possessions over cultivating relationships. Can you imagine how that breaks the heart of God? The children He made in His own image fight to the point of unforgiveness. God sent His Son so that we have the hope of forgiveness and reconciliation through Him. Yet in our hurt, we often turn a deaf ear to God's command to forgive one another.

Joseph's Coat of Many Colors

Adding salt to an open family wound, what does Jacob give Joseph in Genesis 37:3?

Jacob's favoritism is manifested in the form of a coat of many colors. A father giving his son a colorful coat may not seem like a big deal to you and me—today, we can walk into any store and choose from many garments infused with vibrant colors.

What makes this gift so dramatic is that the process of producing color for garments in the ancient world was a very tedious and laborious task. Dyes were exceedingly expensive. Most nomadic garments were black, brown, or perhaps white, but certainly not red, blue, green, or purple.

Joseph's coat had *many* colors, making it an extraordinarily lavish gift from his father. In Jewish culture, such an extravagant gift was usually reserved for the firstborn son.[4] Following that logic, Jacob should have given the coat to Reuben. However, Jacob gives it to Joseph, his *eleventh* son, because Joseph was the firstborn son of his beloved wife Rachel.

If you have siblings, did you ever receive a lavish gift from a parent that caused hard feelings between you and your siblings? If so, what happened?

Children long for love and special attention from their parents. However, it was not a very smart move for Jacob to single out Joseph to such a degree.

Such an obvious sign of favoritism could not be dismissed by Joseph's older brothers.

Some Hebrew scholars believe that the word used here for Joseph's coat is the same word used when describing a garment worn by Tamar, one King David's daughters.

What does 2 Samuel 13:18 say about her garment?

So the garment Jacob gave to Joseph was akin to one worn by royalty. *Ouch.* Jacob was well aware of the damage favoritism could cause because he had experienced it firsthand in his own life.

What does Genesis 25:28 tell us?

Jacob had been his mother's favorite! This, along with the fact that his mother had helped him trick Esau out of his birthright, caused a deep rift between Jacob and his brother. So sibling rivalry and damaging favoritism was nothing new in Joseph's family tree.

In Genesis 27:41, what does Esau vow?

That sounds a whole lot like Joseph and his brothers in Genesis 37:4. The sin of favoritism can cause generational damage.

To be fair, we cannot fault Joseph for his father's lavish gift. He was the recipient, not the giver. However, the coat acted as a lightning rod for the hatred of Joseph's brothers. They directed their hatred toward Joseph, instead of their father, and could not even speak peaceably about him.

As we close today, it is significant to remember that the brothers viewed Joseph's coat as a status symbol within their family. Many years later, God would give Joseph real status, power, and leadership over an entire nation.

We will look at that a little later.

Perhaps Joseph felt loved and secure wearing his father's coat. Perhaps it felt like a refuge from his brothers' ugly behavior toward him. From that place of loss and loneliness, Joseph would eventually learn the truth that God alone is his refuge, security, and protection.

Family strife cuts deep. Family is our flesh and blood, the people who have known us from birth. Above all other people, God designed families to be those who love and protect us the most on earth. Sadly, that is not always the case.

When you and I experience loss and the struggles of this world—especially within our families—we can hold fast to the truth that Jesus knows our pain. He experienced strife and abandonment in His own earthly family. *He understands.*

If family strife has hit you so hard that you feel knocked down and unable to rise, look to the cross. Jesus took those hits to the cross so that one day He will raise us up to Him for all eternity. He alone is our ultimate refuge.

Our most priceless gift.

Go Quiet, Go Deep

Quiet your mind from distractions and pull your Bible close. Bow your head and ask Jesus to make His Word and today's lesson personal for you.

Take your time writing out Psalm 68:19.

What does it mean to you personally that Jesus daily bears us up?

I pray that the boundless love, grace, and forgiveness of Jesus would penetrate every barrier today so that He can work in you and through you.

DAY 2

THE MEANING OF DREAMS

> Now Joseph had a dream, and when he told it to his brothers they hated him even more. (Genesis 37:5)

Sometimes when we have unusual dreams, we tell them to friends or family. Then the game ensues to figure out what they mean. Most of the time, they are humorous dreams—like falling out of bed, being chased by a pumpkin, or running through the town square without a stitch of clothing. However, Joseph's dreams are anything but humorous. In fact, they do not amuse his family one bit.

Read Genesis 37:5–8.

As we learned on Day 1, Joseph's brothers already despise him. Joseph had received an expensive gift from his father in the form of an elaborate coat of many colors. To add insult to injury, Joseph now receives a special gift from his heavenly Father: the ability to interpret dreams.

JOSEPH'S FIRST DREAM

Scripture reveals that God gave Joseph two dreams that related to his own life and four dreams that related to other people's lives. All of them impacted his journey in life-changing ways.

In Genesis 37:6–7, what is Joseph's first dream?

How do his brothers react in Genesis 37:5 and 37:8?

Their reaction is an indication of how much they hate Joseph. They do not think his dream is funny or merely a joke; they are highly offended at the thought of bowing down to "the favorite." However, nearly two decades

23

will pass before Joseph's brothers realize that Joseph's dreams were given by God. In the meantime, they chalk it up to Joseph's presumed inflated self-importance and keep piling on the hate.

Throughout Scripture, God revealed much to His people through dreams. In fact, Joseph's own father, Jacob, received visions and dreams from God.

Read Genesis 28:10–17. What did Jacob dream?

What was the meaning of Jacob's dream?

After waking up, Jacob's first realization was that the Lord was in that place. *That God was with him.* What a beautiful realization when we experience fear. The same holds true for you and me—no matter how scary or intimidating our days or dreams become, God never abandons us. Take a moment to write out these encouraging verses:

Isaiah 41:10

1 John 4:16

What comfort do you find in these verses?

As Joseph's story unfolds, we will see how Joseph knew that God never left him to struggle by his own strength. Even in hard circumstances, Joseph was comforted by that truth.

As I read this account of Joseph's initial dreams, one question screams to the surface: When Joseph's *first* dream does not sit well with his older brothers, why did he share his *second* dream with them? Are you asking that same question?

Perhaps it was simply a self-righteous seventeen-year-old boy's decision. I mean, let's get real; if you have siblings, you have likely been tempted to lord something over them at one point or another.

I have three sisters—one older and two younger. Mom and dad were always very careful to treat us equally to avoid showing favoritism. However, that did not prevent some competition among us in our youth. Like, *I get to play outside because I cleaned my room and you didn't. Na-ne-na-ne-boo-boo!* You get the gist.

However, a more grace-filled view is that Joseph could have been instructed by God to reveal the contents of his prophetic dream. Usually, when God revealed something to one of His prophets, it was meant to be shared for the instruction or blessing of others. This view aligns with Joseph's behavior. However, Scripture is silent as to Joseph's motives.

JOSEPH'S SECOND DREAM
Read Genesis 37:9–11. In Genesis 37:9, what is Joseph's second dream?

Looking back at Joseph's first dream in Genesis 37:6–7, what similarities do you see between Joseph's first and second dreams?

The musical phrase "second verse, same as the first" springs to mind. Here, God is reiterating in a different way the same result: Joseph will one day be elevated in power and prestige above his father and brothers.

Unfortunately, we discover Joseph's inability to read a room at this moment. He shares this second dream with his brothers as well. And for the first time, we see a new emotion enter the narrative: *jealousy*. After the first dream, the brothers "hated him even more" (v. 8). After the second dream, the brothers were "jealous of him" (v. 11). Even today, those two volatile emotions often go hand in hand. One breeds the other and vice versa. And neither yields positive results.

This time around, even Jacob rebukes his son because Joseph's second dream reveals that Jacob as the head of the family (the sun) will *also* bow down one day at Joseph's feet. Not cool.

In their patriarchal society, fathers were given the highest level of respect. In fact, when a family's patriarch walked into a room, it was custom for all the sons to immediately stand. The only exception to that rule was if the father's son became a rabbi. Then the custom would be for the father to rise out of respect for his rabbi son.

For Joseph to be so young and not a rabbi, Jacob found it offensive that Joseph would even suggest that Jacob would bow down before him one day. However, Jacob did one thing that the brothers did not.

What does Genesis 37:11 tell us about Jacob?

Since Jacob himself had been given dreams by God, he likely did not want to rule out that same possibility for his son. Jacob did not like what Joseph's dream revealed, but he could not dismiss it as youthful enthusiasm or sibling rivalry.

Although he never again mentions Joseph's dreams throughout the rest of Genesis, Jacob lived to see those dreams become reality because they were, in fact, from God.

Every dream that God provided various people throughout Scripture came to pass exactly as God revealed. Just as Jacob "kept the saying in mind" with Joseph, similar mindfulness is reflected in Mary's reaction to God revealing that she was the mother of the long-awaited Messiah. What did Mary do in the following verses?

Luke 2:19

Luke 2:51

Where Jacob kept the matter in mind, Mary treasured and pondered the matters in her heart. Taking time to ponder what the Lord is revealing in our lives is a vital step in our spiritual journey.

How long has it been since you took time to carefully seek understanding from the Lord about how He is moving in your life?

Read Proverbs 2:1–11. What stands out to you in these verses?

The only way we can see the way through life is to keep looking up, keep pondering God's beautiful truths, and keep watch for His movements in our life.

What does Psalm 32:8 tell us?

God promises to guide us and give us His counsel. Just as He did with Joseph.

Go Quiet, Go Deep

Quiet your mind from distractions and pull your Bible close. Bow your head and ask Jesus to make His Word and today's lesson personal for you.

Take your time writing out Proverbs 2:1–5.

What does it mean to you personally to keep your heart inclined to Him?

I pray that the boundless love, grace, and forgiveness of Jesus would penetrate every barrier today so that He can work in you and through you.

DAY 3

Journey into the Storm

Now his brothers went to pasture their father's flock near Shechem. And Israel said to Joseph, "Are not your brothers pasturing the flock at Shechem? Come, I will send you to them." And he said to him, "Here I am." So he said to him, "Go now, see if it is well with your brothers and with the flock, and bring me word." So he sent him from the Valley of Hebron, and he came to Shechem. (Genesis 37:12–14)

Our Day 2 lesson left off with Joseph's father and brothers not very pleased with him. The dreams God had given to Joseph had been poorly received by his family. Negative emotions hang in the air like a gray morning mist. So today's lesson finds Joseph taking a road trip from Hebron to Dothan.

Not Just a Day's Journey
Read Genesis 37:12–17. What stands out to you in these verses?

At first glance, we might believe that Jacob simply sends Joseph on a short trip across the fields from their home in Hebron to check on his brothers and flocks. However, Shechem was approximately fifty-three miles from Hebron. *Fifty-three miles.*

It was at least a two-day journey, if not three, and very dangerous for a solo traveler. As a single person, I fully understand the caution that must be taken when traveling alone. But nowadays, we hold the world in the palm of our hands through smartphones. Maps, alerts, and the nearest hotels can all be viewed in a matter of seconds.

The patriarchs, including Abraham and Jacob, were known as pastoralists. They earned their livelihood as shepherds. They were also seminomadic. Instead of moving their tents and encampment every other day, they moved only seasonally in search of water, food, and a good climate for their flocks.

Consequently, Jacob's home in Hebron was a seasonal camp where he stayed in one place and sent his sons out with the flocks in search of pasture and water. With that visual in place, let's pinpoint some key spots along the road of Joseph's journey.

Hebron

Joseph and his family lived in Hebron for generations as sojourners.

Read Genesis 13:14–18. Who settled in Hebron, and what did God promise to him?

In Joseph's story, we see God's promise in action. Jacob was Abraham's grandson and he had twelve sons (Joseph being number eleven). From there, their family tree multiplied exponentially. With Abraham as the spiritual father of all believers, Jew or Gentile, his offspring are truly more numerous than "the dust of the earth" (Genesis 13:16). God kept His promise, indeed.

In this area of Palestine, one of the primary roads for travel and trade was the central ridge route. Basically, the central ridge was the mountainous spine that bridged Shechem in the north all the way to Hebron in the south.

In Genesis 35:27, who gathers at Hebron?

Here we discover that Jacob's grandfather Abraham and father, Isaac, sojourned to Hebron. You might even call their land holding a family plot because it included a burial cave (known as the Cave of the Patriarchs). Abraham's purchase of the parcel of land and Isaac's inheritance of it meant it would remain in the family's possession and not in the possession of the Canaanites. While less common in America, generational family land holdings are common in Israel, Europe, and other parts of the world.

Do you have a home or other gathering place that has been in your family for generations? If so, what memories do you have from there?

My dad's family is from Arkansas. When I was a preteen, we would make an annual summer pilgrimage to attend the Snow Family Reunion along the Buffalo River. More than one hundred Snow relatives and their families would spend a long weekend bonding over lazy canoe rides down the chilly river, swimming and fishing in the crystal-clear water, and enjoying fish and s'mores over the campfires each night.

Those are some of my most cherished childhood memories. It makes me wonder what memories Joseph carried of Hebron.

SHECHEM

Shechem was located in Ephraim's hill county along a pass between Mount Ebal and Mount Gerizim.

According to Genesis 12:6, who stopped in Shechem and why?

Shechem was the first stop of Joseph's great-grandfather Abraham after he entered the land of Canaan in the northern highlands. Abraham had settled there for a time.

According to Genesis 33:18–20, who camped near Shechem and why?

Jacob himself had also camped near Shechem. Therefore, Jacob knew exactly what lay ahead of Joseph as Jacob sent him in search of his brothers.

JOSEPH'S BRAVERY

At the surface of Joseph's journey, it may have seemed like smooth sailing. After all, the only hiccup up to this point was the need to travel a little farther from Shechem to Dothan to actually locate his brothers. However, we would be remiss to not mention Joseph's bravery—even at this early stage.

As his father's favorite, Joseph likely fell under the umbrella of his father's protection. Perhaps Jacob did not know the depth and breadth of the hatred and animosity his ten older sons held against son number eleven.

Perhaps the brothers hid their true feelings any time their father was present. But Joseph knew. And here he was miles from home, miles away from his father's protection, to check on his older brothers and report back. Here, we must ask the obvious: Why did Jacob believe it was necessary to check on his older sons?

Let's bring it closer to home. If you have children at home, why do you feel that it is sometimes prudent to check on them if they have been out of sight for too long? Yes, it could be for safety reasons. However, more often than not, it's because we suspect that they are up to something based on their past behavior. This may be the clue to the answer.

Read Genesis 34:1–7. What happened to Jacob's daughter Dinah?

The consequences of rape, both for the victim and perpetrator, are life-changing. In Old Testament times, women were often considered property that could be bartered to benefit their families. There were no crisis centers, police investigations, or lawyer-laden court trials, of course. The victim's future boiled down to honor. The older brothers knew that their sister had been defiled and sought revenge, even when their father did not.

Read Genesis 34:5–17. How did Jacob's sons respond to the perpetrator's suggestion that their sister, whom he had just defiled, become his wife?

We could not even imagine considering such a scenario today. The perpetrator would be charged, tried, and given prison time. However, the brothers had an ulterior motive behind their suggestion.
What happened in Genesis 34:25–31?

Without consulting their father, Jacob's sons (led by Simeon and Levi) played judge, jury, and executioner. And when their father challenged what they had done, the brothers showed no remorse for willfully deceiving Jacob.

So Jacob had good reason to keep an eye on his older sons. Unfortunately for Joseph, he was apparently one of the tools Jacob used to achieve that purpose.

We leave today's lesson with Joseph successfully locating his brothers at Dothan after a long journey. In other families, such a sibling reunion might have brought smiles and affectionate greetings.

But not Joseph's family. This day would turn out to be one of the most painful in Joseph's entire life.

Thankfully for Joseph, you, and me, God never abandons us on our long journeys or painful days.

Go Quiet, Go Deep

Quiet your mind from distractions and pull your Bible close. Bow your head and ask Jesus to make His Word and today's lesson personal for you.

Take your time writing out 1 Peter 5:10.

What does it mean to you personally that God will restore, confirm, strengthen, and establish you after your suffering?

I pray that the boundless love, grace, and forgiveness of Jesus would penetrate every barrier today so that He can work in you and through you.

DAY 4

LIGHTNING ROD OF HATRED

They saw him from afar, and before he came near to them they conspired against him to kill him. They said to one another, "Here comes this dreamer." (Genesis 37:18–19)

It is not an uncommon occurrence in Scripture to find people plotting to kill one another over positions, possessions, or personal vendettas. And the common denominator in every single one of those situations is that the plotting begins in their minds.

The same is true with you and me. Our actions usually follow our thoughts because our mind informs our limbs. The same is true in spiritual warfare. Victory or defeat often plays out in our minds long before the battle plays out in real time.

That is exactly where we find ourselves in today's lesson. As Joseph approaches his brothers at Dothan to check on them at their father's request, the brothers start scheming.

CONSPIRACY FROM AFAR

Read Genesis 37:18–20.

As the brothers catch a glimpse of Joseph approaching on the horizon, they do not have to guess whether the man is their brother. All they need to see is that coat of many colors catching the sunlight and they dive straight into plotting mode.

In Genesis 37:18, what do the brothers jointly and immediately agree to do?

I don't know about you, but their words are jarring to read. Their unresolved (and likely unconfessed) hatred of Joseph has reached the point where killing him easily becomes their first choice. Not to beat him up. Not to drive him away. They decide to kill him. We can almost feel their venom.

Have you ever had such thoughts? If so, what was the situation? What eventually played out?

I confess that I have had such venomous thoughts in the past. When someone hurts us, our knee-jerk reaction is usually to lash out to make them hurt as much as we do. The deeper the hurt, the more venom we spit back at them. Then we move straight into anger.

It is not wrong to get angry when someone hurts or mistreats us. Even Jesus experienced anger. *Being* angry is not a sin. *Staying* angry can lead us to sin. When we get comfortable in volatile, unresolved anger without confessing or releasing it into the safe hands of our holy God, then sins such as plotting, revenge, and others easily take over. Since our actions follow our thoughts, God reminds us to make every thought captive to Him.

Taking Our Thoughts Captive

The apostle Paul specifically addressed how we are to treat our thoughts in his Second Letter to the believers at Corinth.

Write out 2 Corinthians 10:5.

In your own words, what does "take every thought captive" mean to you?

One of the most common phrases in today's culture is, "Oh, did I just say that out loud?" And usually, whatever that person just said is not uplifting, encouraging, or helpful.

If taking your thoughts captive is a struggle for you, as it sometimes is for me, I have learned a few action points over the years that you may find helpful:

1. *Be accountable to God for your thoughts.* When we keep our thoughts on things above, God will enable us to focus our minds on the right things. God warned Cain about not making this very attitude adjustment. See Genesis 4:7.

2. *Changed thoughts must be accompanied by changed behavior.* In Romans 12:2, Paul urges us to be transformed by the renewing of our minds. A renewed mind is crucial because where the mind goes, the body follows.

3. *Prayer makes all the difference.* Even Paul struggled to do what is good versus what is evil (see Romans 7:15–20). Here, Paul admitted his weaknesses and confessed his sinfulness. He reminds us that looking to and relying on God's strength is crucial.

What harmful or destructive thought can you confess and release to God right now?

Our thoughts can make us or break us. Through the power of the Holy Spirit working in us, we can turn every thought over to Him—the One who empowers us to change our thoughts.

SIN-COVERING LIES

Now that the brothers have agreed to kill Joseph, they start hashing out the details. Here we see a perfect example of what starts in the mind manifesting into action.

In Genesis 37:20, what is the brothers' plan?

Their plan is pretty clear: kill Joseph, get rid of the body, and lie to cover their crime. Like Adam and Eve (and us), their sinful plans include how to hide their sinful behavior. Every time we attempt to hide from God, He always comes looking for us. Not to punish or destroy us, but to restore our fellowship with Him, which was broken by our sin. How do you see that truth in the following verses?

Psalm 139:7–10

Luke 15:8–10

We have a loving God who searches for us and then rejoices with all of heaven when we are found. We have all sinned, fallen short of the glory of God, and sometimes become lost along our journey. Living as people found and redeemed by His grace, love, and mercy is one of life's greatest blessings and witnesses.

PUTTING THEIR PLAN INTO ACTION
Read Genesis 37:21–24.

When the brothers' murderous scheme morphs into action points, Reuben's conscience gets the better of him. So he comes up with a counter-scheme. Notice that Reuben did not object to mistreating Joseph, only to how they would accomplish it. At last, their plotting grows legs.

What two things did the brothers do to Joseph in Genesis 37:23–24?

We may think it odd that their first action is to strip Joseph of his coat of many colors. However, it makes perfect sense. Every time the brothers saw that coat, it reminded them that their father loved someone else more than them—that they were loved less within their own family. *Ouch.* So rather than ripping into Joseph, they rip off the reminder of being loved less.

You and I will experience a lesser love from some people, but we will *never* experience it from God. How do you see that truth in the following verse?

John 3:16

God loved, so He gave. Period. No order of importance required because the ground is level at the foot of the cross.

A Waterless Pit

The second action the brothers take is to throw Joseph into a pit that has no water in it. That is a significant detail. Remember that they are in a dry season. Inhospitable and extremely hot. Water represented the difference between life and death.

In Hebrew, the word *empty* (קֵיר), translated as "vain" or "impoverished," is used over a dozen times in the Old Testament and never in a good light. Whether an empty vessel, soul or state of mind, *empty* points to being void of what is good and life giving. In this case, void of water. For Joseph's brothers to throw him into a waterless pit would guarantee his death.

What is the first sentence in Genesis 37:25?

As if throwing their brother into a waterless pit is not heartless enough, the brothers sit down and consume a meal together. I am not sure how you react to feeling guilty, but I usually get an upset stomach. The very last thing I would be up for is a meal—especially if the reminder of my guilt is within sight or earshot.

However, the brothers' hearts are hardened, and they block out (at least temporarily) their feelings of guilt. They turn a deaf ear to Joseph's cries and enjoy a meal together. It makes me wonder if they ate in silence or chatted jovially at finally ridding themselves of their father's favorite son.

As we close today's lesson, I believe that parents would specifically benefit from taking this part of Joseph's narrative to heart. So much destruction can enter a home when favoritism is allowed to walk through the front door. The resulting jealousy and hurt can destroy the unconditional love and affection within a family. Teaching and demonstrating the unconditional love we receive from God fosters harmony and unity.

You may be experiencing a "pit" season in your life right now. Whether you landed in that pit by someone else's words or actions or threw yourself in, God sees where you have landed.

He has not abandoned you.

I pray that you allow His living water to hydrate and restore you to Him.

Go Quiet, Go Deep

Quiet your mind from distractions and pull your Bible close. Bow your head and ask Jesus to make His Word and today's lesson personal for you.

Take your time writing out Luke 19:10.

What does it mean to you personally that God searches for you when you get lost in your sin?

I pray that the boundless love, grace, and forgiveness of Jesus would penetrate every barrier today so that He can work in you and through you.

DAY 5

SOLD OUT

"Come, let us sell him to the Ishmaelites, and let not our hand be upon him, for he is our brother, our own flesh." And his brothers listened to him. (Genesis 37:27)

How much hatred does it take to turn deaf ears to a family member begging for his life? But that is exactly what Joseph's brothers did. They ripped off Joseph's coat of many colors and threw him into a waterless pit.

A dry cistern in the dry season meant it could be days, weeks, or months before anyone passed by. Joseph was truly in a hopeless position that he was helpless to improve. But his brothers couldn't care less.

THE CALLOUSNESS OF UNREPENTANT SIN
Read Genesis 37:25–28. What stands out to you in those verses?

Because of their cruel indifference, the brothers did not let Joseph's anguish spoil their meal. And what is worse, Joseph's brothers not only heard Joseph begging for his life (see Genesis 42:21) but they also saw the distress of his soul. And still they did not care.

The distress Joseph experienced comes from the Hebrew word *tsarah* (הָרָצ). It is the same word used to describe the distress and grief that Hannah experienced in 1 Samuel 1:6 when the Lord closed her womb. It is beyond momentary sadness or surface distress—it is deep anguish of the soul.

Joseph could do nothing to save himself. Without Jesus, you and I were in a hopeless situation separated from God for all eternity. Yet Jesus volunteered to come down from heaven and pull us out of the dark, waterless pit of hell by shedding His blood to cleanse our sin. How do you see that truth in the following verses?

Romans 5:8

1 John 3:16

1 Peter 3:18

Grace upon grace! Even when life's circumstances throw us into water-less pits, Jesus knows exactly where we have landed. He never abandons us to experience those frightening places alone.

MIDIANITE TRADERS

Perhaps Judah's conscience got the better of him because when he sees the Ishmaelites approaching, he suggests that the brothers sell Joseph rather than shed his blood.

What does he say in Genesis 37:27?

Even though Judah stepped up to save Joseph's life, he stooped down to become a human trafficker. He did not suggest that Joseph's life be saved because of a great love; rather, it was for expediency's sake.

Judah may have proposed selling Joseph to avoid the consequences of being a murderer. Perhaps Judah based his proposal on the moral prohibition of taking his brother's life. Scripture is silent as to his reasons. But it begs a relevant question for us to ponder:

When you feel tempted to sin, do you weigh the consequences of two less-than-stellar options like Judah?

Naturally, the best option is not to sin at all. What do the following passages tell us about sin?

James 4:17

1 John 3:4

1 Corinthians 10:13

Even when we are tempted, God faithfully provides a way out. Perhaps Judah thought he made a better choice by not killing Joseph. However, his second suggestion was just as sinful. Either way, the brothers decide Judah has proposed a good plan and agree. So they sell Joseph to the Ishmaelites.

Here we see another example of how Joseph's life modeled that of Christ.

In Genesis 37:28, how did Joseph's brothers conduct the transaction?

Joseph was sold for twenty pieces of silver. Jesus was sold for thirty pieces of silver. And both were sold by a man named Judas (also spelled Judah).

Little did the brothers realize that they are fulfilling Joseph's dreams with every effort to destroy "the dreamer."

DECEPTION

As far back as Adam in the Garden of Eden, we have attempted to conceal our transgressions. So it is not surprising that Joseph's brothers continue that sinful legacy. As his father's favorite, Joseph would be immediately and greatly missed, so they contrive a story to cover their evil deed.

According to Genesis 37:31–32, what lie did the brothers concoct about Joseph?

They pretend that they randomly happened upon the coat (instead of what they actually did, taking it and dipping it in goat's blood as a ruse), feigning innocence about Joseph showing up to check on them. And when Jacob concludes that Joseph has been torn to bits, the brothers do nothing to correct the misconception; Jacob has responded just as they wanted him to.

When you and I struggle with guilt, we are tempted to allow others to reach wrong conclusions as long as it benefits our purposes too.

What is Jacob's response to Joseph's apparent demise in Genesis 37:34?

If you have experienced the loss of a child, you understand full well Jacob's grief. And for Jacob, it was his favorite child of all, which grieved his heart even deeper.

HEARTLESS COMFORT

There is no comfort as cold as hypocritical comforters. Had they truly cared for their father, they would have offered the truth as comfort. Their selfishness and jealousy prompted them to remain deceitful about Joseph's true location, but they were not without some degree of compassion for their suffering father. Verse 35 tells us, "All his sons and all his daughters rose up to comfort him."

We will never experience such heartless comfort from our Savior. How do you see that truth in the following verses?

Psalm 103:8

Joel 2:13

As we reach the end of Genesis 37, we see that Joseph not only arrived safely in Egypt but also that he was sold as a slave. We will tackle that in our next lesson.

As time would tell, the brothers' involvement and guilt would be made known.

When you and I sin, God sees those sins as we are committing them. Nothing is hidden from our Creator's eyes. Psalm 69:5 says, "The wrongs I have done are not hidden from You." But unlike Joseph's brother Judah whose "rescue" of Joseph was anything but, you and I have the *Lion of Judah* through whom all people are saved.

God does not desire us to be separated from Him one bit, so great is His love for us.

Go Quiet, Go Deep

Quiet your mind from distractions and pull your Bible close. Bow your head and ask Jesus to make His Word and today's lesson personal for you. Take your time writing out Romans 8:1.

What does it mean to you personally that even though you sin, Jesus does not condemn you?

I pray that the boundless love, grace, and forgiveness of Jesus would penetrate every barrier today so that He can work in you and through you.

WEEK 2

POTIPHAR'S HOUSE: GOD'S GRACE AMID DARKNESS

Genesis 39–40

Although he was born with a silver spoon in his mouth, Joseph is now a slave. As he starts his new life in Potiphar's house, God begins molding Joseph into the wise leader he will become. Joseph never asked for that path or such preparation—and sometimes, neither do we.

Yet even on those dark days when we feel cut off from those we love, when the distraction of the familiar is removed, God's grace illuminates the path before us, just as it did for Joseph.

DAY 1 The Lord's Presence *(Genesis 39:1–6a)*

DAY 2 Resisting Temptation *(Genesis 39:6b–20)*

DAY 3 Recognizing the Spirit's Witness *(Genesis 39:21–23)*

DAY 4 Deciphering Dreams *(Genesis 40:1–19)*

DAY 5 Never Forgotten by God *(Genesis 40:20–23)*

KEY QUESTIONS:

- Has God permitted a path that you never dreamed of? What did He show and teach you along the way?

- When it comes to temptation, what is your Achilles' heel?

- What happened when God put you to the test? What did you learn?

- In what impossible situation has God placed you where you learned to trust Him completely?

DAY 1

THE LORD'S PRESENCE

Now Joseph had been brought down to Egypt, and Potiphar, an officer of Pharaoh, the captain of the guard, an Egyptian, had bought him from the Ishmaelites who had brought him down there. The LORD was with Joseph, and he became a successful man, and he was in the house of his Egyptian master. (Genesis 39:1–2)

B efore we dive into Genesis 39, we need to address the apparent diversion from Joseph's narrative in Genesis 38. Some scholars dismiss it as Moses simply spicing up a long narrative. However, nothing could be further from the truth.

AN INTERRUPTION IN THE NARRATIVE

Genesis 37 reveals how Joseph and all of God's people ended up in Egypt rather than Canaan. Chapter 38 reveals God's reasoning behind the Israelites' geographical change. God's people were beginning to intermarry and fall into immorality—particularly Judah, in this chapter. Since our Lord and Savior came from the line of Judah, God needed to maintain the spiritual purity of His people to preserve that lineage. So God removed His children from temptation and sequestered them in the lush surroundings of Goshen.

That is a very brief synopsis of the many important intricacies contained in Genesis 38. If time allows, I encourage you to read through Genesis 38, along with a few commentaries to provide more foundation. However, since our study focuses on Joseph's life, we pick up his narrative again in Genesis 39.

FROM FAVORITE TO SLAVE

Read Genesis 39:1–6a. What stands out to you in these verses?

According to Genesis 39:1, who purchases Joseph? What is his position?

Joseph is taken to Egypt and sold by the Ishmaelites. Similar to the institution in the American South, the economic, military, and political impact of slavery meant that slave trade flourished in Egypt. Slaves were assigned to one of a variety of levels of servitude depending on their ability, land of origin, and social rank. During the sales transaction, it is likely that slaves were probed, prodded, and classified by various standards depending on market needs and clientele. So, even though the transaction is not described in our text, Joseph was undoubtedly frightened, confused, and humiliated.

He could have landed in far worse circumstances, of course. But by God's preordained plan, he is bought by the prominent Egyptian who is in charge of Pharaoh's guard. And that is not all.

The Lord Was with Joseph

The beginning of verse 2 is the key in Joseph's journey, as it is in yours and mine.

Write out Genesis 39:2.

God had a bigger plan than Joseph's current circumstances and never left his side. When you and I land in hard circumstances, it is *never* a surprise to God. Among other benefits, those situations can (1) teach us something new, (2) provide a godly witness to others, or (3) show us a beautiful glimpse of God's love and provision. Sometimes all three happen at once.

When was the last time you landed in a difficult circumstance and found this to be true? What happened?

What did the Lord show or teach you?

How did that allow you to see more of His love and provision?

Take a moment to write out the following verses that reveal God's thoughts and desires toward His children:

Jeremiah 29:11

Matthew 10:29–31

Ephesians 2:10

God is *for* us, never against us! Even when we look around at our circumstances and cannot discern evidence of this, keep these verses close by. Memorize them and let God keep them in your heart. Through them, God will keep your mind on Him despite trials and tribulations.

A WORKER, NOT A WHINER

The Lord was with Joseph and brought him success in Potiphar's house. Did you notice what Joseph did *not* do? Whine. Mumble. Complain. Throw a fit. Take a stance. Joseph trusted God and diligently put his heart and mind to the tasks set before him.

Our culture could give out PhDs in whining, complaining, and taking a stance. Just think back to the pandemic. Or perhaps recall just last week. When we are more concerned about our comfort than glorifying God, our lips start flapping. But not Joseph. His diligent work and can-do attitude brought about a significant revelation.

What does Genesis 39:3 tell us?

Potiphar was Egyptian. There is no scriptural evidence that he followed Yahweh, the one true God. Yet through Joseph's diligent work and the resulting success, Potiphar glimpsed the Almighty. Can you and I say our work ethic provides such a glimpse? There are *many* days that I cannot.

GOD'S HAND AND FAITHFUL WITNESS

God never invited Joseph to His holy drafting table as He created the blueprint of Joseph's life, yet God carefully conceived and carried out every inch of it. (This does not imply that God was responsible for Joseph being enslaved. That was purely the sin of his brothers, which God permitted, then turned to good.)

There is only one reason that anything we do prospers: God. His work in us through the Holy Spirit enables us to do good even when evil resides in our hearts.

God's presence makes the unbearable bearable. Joseph prospered in his new career. God had given Joseph many gifts, which would have never surfaced outside of his new job. Like Joseph, you and I will never discover all that God can do with us as long as we concentrate on only those things we think we are good at. To fulfill God's plan to govern a nation, Joseph needed to learn a whole new culture, country, people skills, management techniques, conflict resolution, and more.

Potiphar was a man of class, wealth, and prestige with qualities and skills Joseph would need.

Sometimes we do not recognize the incubator of learning until God opens the door to release us when the process is complete.

Go Quiet, Go Deep

Quiet your mind from distractions and pull your Bible close. Bow your head and ask Jesus to make His Word and today's lesson personal for you.

Take your time writing out Joshua 1:9.

What does it mean to you personally that the Lord is with you wher-ever you go?

I pray that the boundless love, grace, and forgiveness of Jesus would penetrate every barrier today so that He can work in you and through you.

DAY 2

RESISTING TEMPTATION

Now Joseph was handsome in form and appearance. And after a time his master's wife cast her eyes on Joseph and said, "Lie with me." But he refused and said to his master's wife, "Behold, because of me my master has no concern about anything in the house, and he has put everything that he has in my charge." (Genesis 39:6b–8)

In 2 Samuel 11, we find a familiar story. When King David should have been out in battle with the Israelite army, he opted to stay home instead. He took a leisurely stroll along his rooftop and saw a beautiful woman bathing. And, as the saying goes, he was all in.

The king knew Bathsheba was married, yet it made no difference. He wanted, so he took without regard to God, Uriah, or Bathsheba. What a difference we see in today's lesson.

Read Genesis 39:6b–20. What stands out to you in these verses?

A SLAVE IN POTIPHAR'S HOUSE

Regardless of his diligence and success, Joseph was still a slave. Egyptian slaves in antiquity held few rights. They were merely flesh-and-blood property of their owners.

Some served on farms, working crops or tending livestock. Others worked in more domestic situations like Joseph. Some slaves did hard manual labor, like hauling stones or making bricks for buildings and pyramids. History shows that Egypt relied heavily on slave labor for economic prosperity.[5]

What does Deuteronomy 15:12–15 tell us about slavery?

Joseph was a foreign slave in a foreign land, so the Israelite rule of early release was likely not considered by the Egyptians. Joseph could have been Potiphar's slave for life. And although Joseph was successful in that role, God had other plans.

POTIPHAR'S WIFE

Just when we think Joseph's situation as a slave may be improving, a phrase of impending doom appears in the narrative.

Write out the last sentence of Genesis 39:6.

Novelists would classify this sentence as foreshadowing. It is a literary device that indicates suspense and drama looming on the horizon. In the very next sentence, Potiphar's wife slithers in from stage left.

In Genesis 39:7, what does Potiphar's wife do?

In today's vernacular, she gave Joseph *the eye*. What follows is what I believe to be one of the most sinister seductions in Scripture, apart from the seducement of Adam and Eve by the serpent and the attempted seducement of Jesus by Satan.

Now, having worked with labor and employment law attorneys for three decades, I can verify the actions of Potiphar's wife would have been a clear-cut case of sexual harassment. However, since slaves did not have modern-day rights, Joseph gets railroaded by circumstantial evidence.

FLEEING SIN (LITERALLY)

When temptation came knocking in the form of Potiphar's wife, Joseph resisted it with a vengeance. Without ever knowing the apostle Paul on earth, Joseph lived out what Paul teaches us in 1 Corinthians.

Write out 1 Corinthians 10:13.

Even though we feel that sin has been targeted directly at us, the enemy uses the same temptations on many people.

Satan often tempts us in our strength because he knows that in that arena, we tend to be self-reliant—like Peter's confidence that he would never deny Jesus. When he should have prayed for strength, he slept instead.

Have you experienced and fallen into a temptation where you thought you were strong? If so, what happened?

Sometimes our resistance makes a bad situation worse. Joseph's resistance to temptation was met with false accusations and unjust imprisonment. Yet Joseph would never be sorry that he honored God and Potiphar with his choice.

FROM SLAVERY TO PRISON

As a slave in a foreign land, with no way to defend himself, Joseph was thrown into a dungeon without voice, vote, or even a lawyer.

Even though we would never volunteer for such incarceration, many blessings come when God allows challenging situations in our lives.

This reminds me of the apostle Paul again. He was spreading the Gospel message far and wide, and he kept ending up in prison. In fact, Paul wrote his Letter to the Philippians while under house arrest in Rome.

Paul may have been tempted to complain, argue his innocence, or even get angry with God about the mission trips he was unable to take. However, the Book of Philippians is known as the book of joy. Joy from prison? You bet.

What did Paul say in Philippians 4:8?

Can you remember a time when you initially thought your situation had gone from bad to worse, only to discover later how powerfully God used

that time in your life? If so, what happened?

How did that experience increase your faith?

The Lord Was Still with Joseph

God is with us each moment of every day to bring good out of evil. Situations such as the ones that Joseph and Paul endured allow us to learn what is utterly impossible with man is absolutely possible with God.

Yet even though Joseph made the right decision to honor God by fleeing from Potiphar's wife, his situation deteriorated.

Have you experienced a situation where you made the right choice, but things seemed to get worse? If so, what happened?

What did God reveal to you through that process?

When situations do not go as we plan, or when we take the high road but feel punished like a criminal, it is easy to fall into despair or even hopelessness. However, God promises that nothing will touch our lives that has not been through His hands first.

Whatever comes into our lives, no matter how painful, God has a purpose to bring beauty from the ashes. And the beauty that emerges is far more spectacular than anything we could have hoped for or imagined.

Go Quiet, Go Deep

Quiet your mind from distractions and pull your Bible close. Bow your head and ask Jesus to make His Word and today's lesson personal for you.

Take your time writing out James 1:2–3.

What does it mean to you personally that God will faithfully provide perseverance when you face all kinds of trials in life?

I pray that the boundless love, grace, and forgiveness of Jesus would penetrate every barrier today so that He can work in you and through you.

DAY 3

Recognizing the Spirit's Witness

And Joseph's master took him and put him into the prison, the place where the king's prisoners were confined, and he was there in prison. But the LORD was with Joseph and showed him steadfast love and gave him favor in the sight of the keeper of the prison. (Genesis 39:20–21)

It is a common belief in our culture that if we do the right thing, good things will automatically happen. When we help someone and do a good deed, somewhere in the back of our minds, we believe that we are due good in return. Like it's owed to us.

However, the true test happens when we do the right thing, even when no one is watching. Whether people see our good deeds, God does not miss a single one. And that is where we find ourselves in Joseph's story.

The Lord Was Still with Joseph
Read Genesis 39:21–23. What stands out to you in those verses?

Despite Joseph's situation declining from slavery to prisoner, the transition begins with a clear reminder that God is with Joseph. Still. He never left his side, not for a moment. In fact, Genesis 39:21 goes even further to reveal that God showed Joseph steadfast love.

What is the first thing that comes to mind when you hear about God's steadfast love?

Why, in particular?

All children long to hear that their father loves them. There's an infinite sense of belonging and security in a father's unconditional love. And how much more that increases when we hear that our heavenly Father loves us!

He who knitted us together in our mother's womb delights in loving us. He *chose* us. Take time to write out these relevant verses:

Jeremiah 1:5

John 15:16

Isaiah 43:1

What is your response to the Lord's all-consuming love for you?

Reading Genesis 39:21 in many other versions shows the consistent love and blessing of God:

- "The Lord was with him. He was kind to him." (NIrV)
- "But the Lord was with Joseph in the prison and showed him his faithful love." (NLT)
- "But the Lord was with Joseph and showed him mercy." (NKJV)
- "But the Lord was with Joseph and blessed him." (GNT)
- "But *Adonai* was with Yosef, showing him grace." (CJB)

Our souls long to hear and receive those things from our heavenly Father:

kindness, faithful love, mercy, blessing, and grace. We may not hear such words regularly on earth, but God sings them over us every day.

Each and every day, you and I receive all of those wonderful blessings from the Lord. Take time to write out the following verses, and then read them aloud to yourself:

Psalm 67:6–7

Lamentations 3:22–23

1 John 3:1

Regardless of how we perceive that others love us, the Creator of the universe loves us so much that He sent His Son to die in our place. We will never taste spiritual death because, in Christ, we have an eternal inheritance. Read those passages again. Take a moment here to thank God for such lavish, unconditional love.

PRISONER EXTRAORDINAIRE

God not only gave Joseph faithful love, kindness, mercy, blessing, and grace through His presence but He also granted Joseph divine favor with the keeper of the prison. There is a connection here with Potiphar that we need to note.

According to Genesis 39:1, what is Potiphar's job under Pharaoh?

According to Genesis 39:20, in what prison was Joseph placed?

As captain of Pharaoh's (the king's) guard, Potiphar also served as the ultimate overseer of the king's prison. Any slave accused of Joseph's crime should have been executed. The fact that Potiphar spared Joseph's life and put him in a prison under his watchful care reveals that perhaps Potiphar did not fully believe his wife's account of what transpired.

Potiphar and his household had benefitted greatly from Joseph's administrative gifts. It is not a stretch to imagine Potiphar putting in a good word on Joseph's behalf to the keeper of the prison. It would certainly reflect well on Potiphar if his prison were run as smoothly and efficiently as his house had been under Joseph's care.

When you and I are faithful with what God puts in front of us—regardless of our surroundings—He will bless the work of our hands.

If you find yourself in trying circumstances today, keep the words of Colossians 3:23 close: "Whatever you do, work heartily, as for the Lord and not for men."

May God bless the work of your diligent hands today for His glory.

Go Quiet, Go Deep

Quiet your mind from distractions and pull your Bible close. Bow your head and ask Jesus to make His Word and today's lesson personal for you.

Take your time writing out Ephesians 6:7.

What does it mean to you personally to work for God and not man?

I pray that the boundless love, grace, and forgiveness of Jesus would penetrate every barrier today so that He can work in you and through you.

DAY 4

DECIPHERING DREAMS

And one night they both dreamed—the cupbearer and the baker of the king of Egypt, who were confined in the prison—each his own dream, and each dream with its own interpretation. (Genesis 40:5)

Although I have never been locked in a prison, I know people who have. The last thought in their minds is how they can be helpful to those incarcerated around them. Their minds are usually occupied with shame, regret, guilt, and finding ways to be released as soon as possible.

As we pick up Joseph's story, he has spent time behind bars. Now in his late twenties, he probably had pictured a different life path than his current situation. As a favorite son in a prosperous, patriarchal family, prison time had likely never crossed his mind. Yet here he was.

Rather than complain and fall into despair, Joseph puts his God-given administrative gifts to use that he honed while serving Potiphar. And one day, two new prisoners appear behind bars.

Read Genesis 40:1–19. What stands out to you in these verses?

First and foremost, Genesis 40:3 confirms that the prison where Joseph and these two officials were kept fell under Potiphar's authority as captain of the guard. Like so many other bosses, perhaps Potiphar realized that people with extraordinary administrative gifts are hard to find. Since Joseph could no longer organize Potiphar's home (thanks to his wife), Joseph was moved to organize Potiphar's prison.

THE FIRST PRISONER: CHIEF CUPBEARER

The first prisoner mentioned is the chief cupbearer of the king of Egypt. He was certainly not your run-of-the-mill prisoner. The text does not provide a reason for his incarceration but only his position in Pharaoh's household.

This is the first time that the position of cupbearer appears in Scripture. However, there is a cupbearer we may be more familiar with in the Old Testament.

According to Nehemiah 1:11, who was the cupbearer to the king?

In Nehemiah 2:1, what is one of the functions of the cupbearer?

Here, *cupbearer* (הַקְשֶׁמ) means "one giving drink." However, the biblical term *cupbearer* is also used in the context of a butler. In fact, when the cupbearer in Joseph's prison is mentioned later in Genesis 40:21, the King James Version says: "And he restored the chief butler unto his butlership again; and he gave the cup into Pharaoh's hand."

Consequently, a cupbearer's position carried far greater responsibilities than merely tasting the king's wine to ensure it was not poisoned. Since royal courts were usually rife with plots and intrigues, a cupbearer must be trustworthy above all. Such a proprietary and confidential relationship often endeared cupbearers to their kings, and the cupbearers often received influential positions in gratitude. *The Lutheran Study Bible* provides this insight regarding both the cupbearer and the baker:

> High Egyptian court officials with authority over the drinks and
> food of Pharaoh's household. Besides handling these official du-
> ties, they often were influential in the royal court.[6]

The fact that the cupbearer in Joseph's prison was designated as "chief cupbearer" indicates that there were others in that position with one chief to hold them accountable. This was a man of great importance and influence in Pharaoh's court.

THE SECOND PRISONER: CHIEF BAKER

The second prisoner mentioned is the chief baker of the king of Egypt. Again, not your ordinary prisoner and no reason is provided for his prison confinement.

In antiquity, a royal court's baker was not merely a pastry chef; rather, he was usually a head chef who was responsible for preparing high-quality meals for the king and his household (and often their courtiers as well). A chief baker also carried influence in large part because of the purchasing power for food and goods, as well as employing other cooks to serve under him.

Since both the chief cupbearer and chief baker were responsible for Pharaoh's wine and food, their offenses may well have been neglecting to provide the best of either, which drew royal wrath. And while they were in prison, both had troublesome dreams.

What does Joseph ask them in Genesis 40:7?

Joseph actually *saw* the prisoners. This provides us an important glimpse at Joseph's compassionate heart. Most prisoners are downcast, but he noticed that these two prisoners were particularly troubled. Perhaps Joseph recognized it because he himself was unjustly imprisoned.

In our fast-paced culture, we do not often slow down long enough to notice a mere acquaintance's countenance. Beyond a quick nod and a standard greeting, we usually keep walking right past them. What do the following verses tell us about compassion?

1 Peter 3:8

Colossians 3:12

The very first book I wrote was called *The God of All Comfort*. It was born out of the desire to fight the apathy I felt in our culture—and still feel. The entire Bible study centered on 1 Corinthians 1:3–7.

Read 1 Corinthians 1:3–7. What two attributes of God are mentioned in verse 3?

God not only offers all comfort but He also is the Father of compassion. As Christ-followers, we are to be like Him. I truly believe that you and I feel His holy compassion and want to comfort others, but our hectic schedules interrupt intentional follow-through.

I challenge you (and myself, as I look in the mirror), that the next time the Lord moves you to compassion and gives clear leading to comfort someone who is hurting, you would commit to following the Lord's leading at that very moment.

THE CUPBEARER'S DREAM

Take a moment to reread Genesis 40:9–13.

Appropriately, the cupbearer's dream includes grapevines and performing the tasks of his former position.

What did Joseph's dream interpretation reveal to the cupbearer?

The cupbearer is greatly relieved to hear that his circumstances will improve. When you believe the worst is coming, hearing that you will be restored feels like a rush of life-giving oxygen in an atmosphere of suffocating despair.

Have you experienced a similar feeling? How did God encourage you in the feeling?

After Joseph finishes interpreting the cupbearer's dream, what does he ask the cupbearer to do in Genesis 40:14?

And in Genesis 40:23, what does the cupbearer do?

It is interesting that the cupbearer never promised Joseph that he would speak to Pharaoh on Joseph's behalf. Perhaps he wanted to see if Joseph's interpretation accurately came to pass. Perhaps the cupbearer was self-centered and never had any intention of mentioning Joseph to the king if he was freed. We can only speculate. However, if you have ever been let down by someone you thought would help you but who didn't come through, you can relate to what Joseph may have felt at this point.

THE BAKER'S DREAM

Now it's the chief baker's turn. He hears that Joseph's interpretation of the chief cupbearer's dream was favorable, so he rushes to tell Joseph his dream.

Read Genesis 40:16–19. What did Joseph's dream interpretation reveal to the baker?

Ouch. That is probably the very opposite of what the baker wanted to hear. Nevertheless, the baker is in the same boat as the cupbearer: nothing has happened *yet*. At this point, they do not know if Joseph's interpretations will come to fruition.

HONEST INTERPRETATIONS

We need to pause and notice an often-overlooked aspect of Joseph's interpretations of the cupbearer's and baker's dreams. Joseph did not interpret their dreams to benefit himself. He did not interpret them in a way that would give those two men false hope just to ease their fears. He gave them the *true* interpretations that the Lord gave to him.

Throughout Scripture, one specific thing differentiates a false prophet from a true prophet of God. A false prophet always provides an interpretation that the people want to hear. God's true prophets always give precise interpretations to the people even if the news is bad. Simply read through the stories of Jeremiah and Isaiah.

How often do you and I tend to manipulate our circumstances in an attempt to steer the outcomes for our own benefit? Joseph could have easily told the cupbearer and baker that their circumstances were temporary, and they would both be wreathed in good fortune after their immediate release from prison. Joseph remained true to God and gave the baker's true dream interpretation, even though it was bad news.

Joseph chose to faithfully follow the Lord without regard for his personal comfort or benefit. And God would bless Joseph exceedingly for such steadfast faithfulness.

Go Quiet, Go Deep

Quiet your mind from distractions and pull your Bible close. Bow your head and ask Jesus to make His Word and today's lesson personal for you.

Take your time writing out Matthew 9:36.

What does it mean to you personally that Jesus sees your suffering and has compassion for you?

I pray that the boundless love, grace, and forgiveness of Jesus would penetrate every barrier today so that He can work in you and through you.

DAY 5

NEVER FORGOTTEN BY GOD

On the third day, which was Pharaoh's birthday, he made a feast for all his servants and lifted up the head of the chief cupbearer and the head of the chief baker among his servants. He restored the chief cupbearer to his position, and he placed the cup in Pharaoh's hand. But he hanged the chief baker, as Joseph had interpreted to them. Yet the chief cupbearer did not remember Joseph, but forgot him. (Genesis 40:20–23)

In high school, I absolutely loved being in the band. We spent a lot of time together rehearsing, playing for pep rallies, playing school fight songs at football games, marching at halftime, and traveling to various competitions. So fun! During one particular game when I was a junior, our football team won a huge victory over our rival school. Let the after-game celebration begin!

All of my closest friends were also in the band, and all of our parents knew one another, so my friends and I were constantly at one another's homes for various activities, to study, or to just hang out. They were safe, welcoming spaces.

That evening, the after-game pizza band party had been set at John Allen's house. The buses returned to school after the game around 11:00 p.m., and the band members went their separate ways to get to the party.

Somehow, my parents thought I had secured a ride with one of my friends. And I thought my parents were picking me up from school with frozen pizzas to contribute to the party. Standard procedure on previous occasions. Except for that night.

By midnight I was the only student still sitting outside in the dark waiting for a ride. Cell phones did not exist in 1985. Even though the school was in a safe neighborhood, it was midnight, and I was alone. Fear and feelings of abandonment overwhelmed me.

When the assistant band director finally left to lock up the school and go home, he found me still waiting and in tears. He was a very kind man, so he talked me out of hysterics and took me to the party (leaving only after he confirmed that my parents were there).

When I walked in trying to appear calm, I realized that neither my parents nor my friends had yet noticed my absence. No one was looking for me. My teenage melodramatics took it from there. I burst into tears and my parents felt terrible. Suffice it to say, such an incident never repeated itself.

Even today, I clearly remember that hour when I sat outside, waiting in the dark. Every time a car pulled in to pick up a bandmate, I looked up, hoping to see my parents. After an hour, I stopped looking up. Hope had left the building.

Now imagine Joseph. He asked the cupbearer to remember him when the cupbearer was released from prison. I can easily picture Joseph waiting in the dark. For hours and days, every time he heard footsteps approaching his prison cell, he likely looked up in the hope of deliverance. But Joseph had to wait two years; he probably just stopped looking up when he heard footsteps.

Still, Joseph never stopped trusting God and looking up to the Lord for deliverance. Even though no one was looking to rescue him, Joseph kept the faith. His hope in God never left the building. What a beautiful example for you and me when darkness threatens to overwhelm us.

Read Genesis 40:20–23. What stands out to you in these verses?

INTERPRETATION VERIFICATION

We open up today's lesson at Pharaoh's birthday party. And the first few words are these: "On the third day."

According to Genesis 40:13 and 40:19, how many days did Joseph tell the cupbearer and baker would pass before their heads were lifted up?

Here, we see Joseph's dream interpretations beginning to reveal their accuracy. Joseph predicted that in three days, each of the two would be released from prison. It makes me wonder if the cupbearer and baker noticed that those interpretations were beginning to unfold right before their eyes.

Scripture does not reveal if the cupbearer and baker were released in time to actually prepare any of Pharaoh's celebratory food and drink, but only that he lifted them up among his other servants. However, each of them would soon be singled out for very different reasons.

In Genesis 40:21, what did Pharaoh do to the chief cupbearer?

In Genesis 40:22, what did Pharaoh do to the chief baker?

Both men's sentences happened exactly as Joseph had interpreted. The cupbearer was restored, and the baker was hanged. It would be hard to believe that either of those men forgot Joseph's interpretations as events unfolded.

Has anyone ever predicted how a future event would unfold in your life, and they turned out to be exactly right? If so, what was the situation? What happened?

Such specificity has not happened to me, though certain friends have generally stated over the years that they could see God moving me into full-time ministry one day. That has now come to fruition, but those general statements do not compare with the direct dream interpretations that God gave to Joseph.

FORGOTTEN IN PRISON

As Joseph waited in prison, he asked only one thing from the cupbearer:

that he remember Joseph when he was released.

What happened in Genesis 40:23?

Now that the cupbearer was free and his life was running smoothly again, he promptly forgot Joseph. It could be that the cupbearer honestly did not recall Joseph's request to remember him to Pharaoh. Or it could be that the cupbearer did not want to remind Pharaoh that he had once said or done something that invoked Pharaoh's wrath for fear of a repeat event. We do not know which is true. We simply know that the cupbearer forgot Joseph.

Has someone ever promised you a great favor only to leave you disappointed? If so, what happened?

Did you ever bring up that disappointment to the person who made the promise?

Throughout the rest of Joseph's narrative, we never see Joseph seeking out the cupbearer to demand an apology for leaving him in prison. He never sent troops to throw the cupbearer back in prison for his memory lapse either. But we will see that through Joseph's life, forgiveness was his standard pattern and practice.

One Saved, One Condemned

In the cupbearer's and baker's stories, we see a resemblance between Joseph and Jesus. Joseph's situation with two men played out in a prison. Jesus' story with two other men played out on a cross.

Read Luke 23:32–43.

Two criminals were crucified on either side of Jesus. One criminal

69

derided Jesus and made fun of His claims to be God. But not the other one.
In Luke 23:42, what does the second criminal ask Jesus?

Simply this: *remember me*. The first criminal was condemned. The second criminal was saved. Joseph's request to be remembered by the cupbearer fell on deaf ears. The criminal's request to be remembered by Jesus fell on holy ears.

When you and I lift our hearts in prayer, it is Jesus' holy ears that hear our requests. We do not have to ask Him to remember us. He loves us with such a holy passion that He died in our place. He never forgets us. *Ever.*

Yet how often do we forget Jesus? In our darkest moments when we promise to be faithful and follow Him in all things, do we remember our promises when the light reappears?

We never have to wonder if Jesus remembers us or His promises to us. Beginning with salvation and ending with resurrection into eternity with Him by grace and faith alone, He faithfully honors every single promise He ever made to us.

Every.

Single.

One.

Go Quiet, Go Deep

Quiet your mind from distractions and pull your Bible close. Bow your head and ask Jesus to make His Word and today's lesson personal for you.

Take your time writing out Psalm 27:10.

What does it mean to you personally that even though people may forget you, Jesus never will?

I pray that the boundless love, grace, and forgiveness of Jesus would penetrate every barrier today so that He can work in you and through you.

WEEK 3

FROM PRISON TO PROMINENCE

Genesis 41

When Potiphar threw Joseph in prison, God could have liberated him in an instant. But God knew that beyond this battle, a war was coming in the form of a devastating famine. Joseph needed to develop godly strength, hone extraordinary administrative gifts, and learn to wholeheartedly trust in the Lord in every circumstance.

God knew it was better for Joseph to lose that battle and win the coming war. God had a far greater purpose for Joseph than vindicating him from false imprisonment. God would use Joseph to rescue His chosen people from death.

DAY 1   Pharaoh's Dreams (*Genesis 41:1–7*)

DAY 2   Only God Can Interpret Dreams (*Genesis 41:8–36*)

DAY 3   Joseph's Rise to Power (*Genesis 41:37–45*)

DAY 4   Plentiful Gathering (*Genesis 41:46–52*)

DAY 5   Persevering in Hardship (*Genesis 41:53–57*)

KEY QUESTIONS:

- Do you think God is angry with you if you do not understand the meaning or reason behind the hardships you face?

- Have you noticed that God matures your gifts over time for His purposes?

- As you land in life's pits and prisons, are you still a shining witness that God is with you no matter what?

DAY 1

PHARAOH'S DREAMS

After two whole years, Pharaoh dreamed that he was standing by the Nile. (Genesis 41:1)

One of the greatest tests one can ever hope to pass—before being greatly used by God—is to be misunderstood and then punished even after doing the right thing. (And keeping our mouths humbly shut about any earthly mistreatment.)

Joseph was punished by Potiphar for what his wife claimed was attempted rape. Despite the fact that he did everything right in the eyes of God by literally fleeing from sin, Joseph was unceremoniously thrown into prison. Yet even in prison, Joseph had not sugarcoated or hidden the unfavorable interpretation of the baker's dream in hope of gaining favor. Joseph trusted God above all and clung to His promises.

As we dig into the third chapter of this study, we begin in the same place as Joseph—clinging to the truth that everything God forecasted and promised will come true.

Write out Matthew 24:2, 34.

After predicting the destruction of the temple, Jesus said that Peter would deny Him. That Judas would betray Him. That He would be raised on the third day to take His heavenly place as our eternal mediator. That He has prepared a place for all believers in heaven. God is at work! God's purpose for us far exceeds any prison in which we land. Now let's dive back into Joseph's narrative.

Read Genesis 41:1–7. What stands out to you in these verses?

Two More Years in Prison

The first few words of Genesis 41 reveal that Joseph had spent two more years in prison after the cupbearer forgot him. We can only imagine how Joseph may have struggled to cling to hope for rescue. This is a vivid reminder of how much you and I need patience—not simply the strength to endure testing, but the patience to wait and trust the Lord's timing.

What does Psalm 105:16–20 tell us?

In this passage, King David specifically refers to Joseph's patience in trusting God, His timing, and His promises. Joseph patiently waited without complaint until God's deliverance from prison came to pass. Waiting for God's timing is one of the hardest disciplines for faithful believers. But it is worth the wait!

In your life, what have you specifically waited for over a long period of time?

Are you still waiting? If so, how is your patience level?

Waiting with patience is a constant struggle in our lightning-fast culture. Patience feels like a never-ending clash against our carefully planned calendars. That waiting time is a humbling reminder of who is truly in charge. There is one verse that I have gravitated toward for years that has helped every single time that I have struggled to be patient.

Write out Habakkuk 2:3.

If it seems slow, wait for it. Just wait. If you struggle with patiently waiting on God's timing, write this verse in the margin next to Genesis 41:1. Write it on sticky notes and put them where you have a constant visual reminder of God's faithfulness and matchless timing.

When God moves in our lives after an extended waiting period, we ultimately realize that He moved at the absolute perfect time. God faithfully strengthens and prepares us in life's pits and prisons for His eternal purposes. Joseph waited and was rewarded more than he could have possibly hoped or imagined.

PHARAOH'S DREAMS

Even though I'm from Texas, I have never dreamed about cows. Horses, yes. Cows? No. However, cows were an important part of ancient Egypt's survival and economy. Dating as far back as 4500 BC, tomb scenes depict the importance of cattle in ancient Egypt. They provided food, leather for clothes and goods, and vital agricultural uses such as plowing. So it shouldn't surprise us that Pharaoh's dreams included cattle and agriculture.

According to Genesis 41:1–4, what was Pharaoh's first dream?

According to Genesis 41:5–7, what was Pharaoh's second dream?

It is easy to see why Pharoah was troubled. The dreams are a bit creepy. In fact, the dreams were so vivid that when Pharaoh awoke, he was so shaken it took him a moment to realize that they were, in fact, dreams.

Have you ever had a dream so vivid that you woke up shaken? If so, what was the dream about? What came out of it?

75

I have had only one such vivid dream where I can still recall every single detail. In 2010, I experienced a heartbreaking divorce. Everything in my life was shaken, and I often felt attacked—by Satan, by the fallout of my ex-husband's actions, by friends who chose to fade into the shadows, and by a secular court system.

I sought counseling from my senior pastor's wife, who is a licensed Christian counselor. A few months into the whole divorce ordeal, I sat in my weekly counseling appointment with Kristin. The night before that appointment, I'd had a dream that troubled me deeply and, frankly, creeped me out.

In my dream, I woke up to find my house filled with snakes. Snakes of all shapes, colors, and sizes covered the floor and furniture. They hung from ceiling fans, draped over the doors, and sat coiled on windowsills. I could not even see the floor due to the sheer number of snakes. And their slitted eyes were all focused on my every move.

I leaped out of bed and bolted through the snakes to the back door. As I ran, the snakes struck out at me from above and below. As I opened the back door to run outside, even more snakes greeted me. They were draped over the fence, slithered through the grass, and coiled on lawn chairs.

I screamed my head off and woke up. The moment I woke up, I frantically looked around my bedroom for any snakes. Any hint of a hiss. All was well, but I was very rattled.

Although that dream (in my opinion) had nothing to do with the reason I was seeking counseling, it unnerved me to such a degree that I relayed the dream to Kristin. She asked one simple question that I truly believe was straight from the heart of God: "Did any of the snakes actually get you?"

Stunned by her question, I had to think back. Not one snake had actually made contact with me. And Kristin profoundly stated, "God is reminding you that He's protecting you." That proved to be a significant turning point in my healing process.

If you are feeling attacked in this season of life, take heart. You and I will have snakes in all shapes and forms strike at us while we walk on earth. Satan and his legions will watch your every move through slitted eyes. But God is your impenetrable protector! God alone is your mighty fortress, safe refuge, and ultimate snake-crusher! In those moments when you feel attacked, remember this: focus on your Savior, not on your snakes.

GOD IS ON THE MOVE

The implications of Joseph's story contain the beauty of the Gospel message. In God's perfect wisdom and timing, He allowed Joseph to experience fiery trials to equip and raise up a godly leader. When we rely on God's perfect timing by faith, He never disappoints.

What does Romans 5:6 tell us?

Regardless of the fiery trials or times of suffering we endure, God still promises to save all who believe by faith that Jesus died for our sin, was raised from the dead, and has gone to prepare a place for us in heaven.

Enduring severe trials like Joseph is not a prerequisite for salvation. Yet as God leads through our fires and we watch Him resurrect beauty from ashes, the Spirit builds our faith—a gift to cherish.

Go Quiet, Go Deep

Quiet your mind from distractions and pull your Bible close. Bow your head and ask Jesus to make His Word and today's lesson personal for you.

Take your time writing out John 13:7.

What does it mean to you personally that even though you may experience impatience when you cannot understand how the Lord is working, being in God's presence one day will be enough?

I pray that the boundless love, grace, and forgiveness of Jesus would penetrate every barrier today so that He can work in you and through you.

DAY 2

ONLY GOD CAN INTERPRET DREAMS

So in the morning his spirit was troubled, and he sent and called for all the magicians of Egypt and all its wise men. Pharaoh told them his dreams, but there was none who could interpret them to Pharaoh. (Genesis 41:8)

W e looked at Pharaoh's two dreams in our Day 1 lesson. And here we see that Pharaoh's two startling dreams troubled his spirit. Let's admit it, they were kind of creepy, right? Emaciated cows eating plump cows. Eww. Pharaoh could not shake his troubled feelings, so he gathered all of Egypt's magicians and wise men to interpret his dreams. And the story's drama gains momentum.

THE CUPBEARER'S CONFESSION

Read Genesis 41:8–13. What stands out to you in these verses?

No one could interpret Pharaoh's dreams. Is it any wonder? The dreams came from Yahweh, and Pharaoh's interpreters did not know Yahweh. But there was a man that God kept secure not far away who knew about both God and dreams. At that moment, we can almost smell Joseph's liberation. And like a blast from the past, the cupbearer again enters from stage left.

In Genesis 41:9, what are the cupbearer's first words to Pharaoh?

The cupbearer begins his conversation with Pharaoh by confessing his offense. Knowing that the cupbearer remained silent for two years before this points to the probability that he was more interested in garnering Pharaoh's favor than offering genuine gratitude to Joseph. But to his credit, he begins with confession.

Have you ever begun a conversation with a confession? If so, what was the occasion?

When we have neglected a friend or forgotten a significant event in a loved one's life, repentance is an excellent place to start. Confession and repentance acknowledge that we have slighted someone or caused offense in some way, whether intentionally or not.

Confession is a vital part of our relationship with our Savior. In prayer, when we confess our sins, shortcomings, and offenses against the Lord, He clears our account with loving forgiveness. We may not always receive that from people, but we always receive it from Jesus.

After his confession, the chief cupbearer tells Pharaoh about a "young Hebrew" who interpreted both his and the chief baker's dreams and how events unfolded exactly how the young man had interpreted.

In this moment, we see God's hand again in Joseph's situation. Had the cupbearer brought Joseph to Pharaoh's attention when he was first released two years before, Joseph would have likely gone back home. Perhaps, had he been a nomadic shepherd, Joseph would have been hard to locate when Pharoah needed him. So God, in His perfect wisdom, kept Joseph in prison so Pharaoh knew exactly where to find him.

Make no mistake: Joseph's time in prison was not a pleasant experience. But then, God never promises pleasantness to any of us in life. He never promises us a bed of roses. He promises something infinitely more priceless: His presence in and with us. Pause and write out these beautiful reminders:

John 14:16–17

Matthew 28:20

Emmanuel—God with us. He lives in every believer. He is the fire in our soul. He is the peace in our minds. He is *everything* we need in *every* circumstance. And He was with Joseph, never leaving him for a moment.

JOSEPH SUMMONED BEFORE PHARAOH

The cupbearer's story to Pharaoh was not hearsay but an eyewitness account and personal experience. Eureka! Pharaoh wasted no time in summoning Joseph. Such haste demonstrates just how much Pharaoh's two dreams had troubled him. A Hebrew prisoner was likely not a common source for such a task, but Pharaoh wanted answers. And pronto.

Read Genesis 41:14. What is the first thing that Joseph does when he is liberated?

Proper grooming was not usually a priority in prison. It was customary for Jewish men to have beards; however, Egyptians were typically clean shaven. It is interesting that each time Joseph changes location in his saga, clothes are part of the story.

He began as a favorite son with a coat of many colors that was literally ripped off him by jealous brothers. Then he was a successful overseer of Potiphar's house (which likely required a better-than-average wardrobe, part of which was ripped off him by Potiphar's wife). Then Joseph sported prison garb after being accused of attempted rape. Now here, Joseph again changes clothes to don something presentable for Pharaoh (see Genesis 41:14). Clothing has historically been used to display position, wealth, and influence. Joseph's wardrobe would continue to improve for the rest of his life.

Read Genesis 41:15–16.

Joseph was brought to Pharaoh. He was likely surprised by the quick sequence of events (much like Peter in Acts 12:9 when the angel liberated him from prison). And in very short order, Joseph finds himself face-to-face with the most powerful man in the land.

JOSEPH RIGHTLY GIVES HONOR TO GOD

God resurfaces Joseph's gift of dream interpretation for the third time, and we see how God has caused Joseph to mature. When Joseph interpreted his dreams to his brothers, he neglected to read the hostility of his audience in the room. When Joseph interpreted the cupbearer's and baker's dreams, he remained in prison for another two years.

Now the stakes are high. Pharaoh tells Joseph he has heard Joseph can interpret dreams. Perhaps worst-case scenario images raced through Joseph's mind at this point. Yet Joseph trusts God once again.

In Genesis 41:16, what does Joseph say to Pharaoh?

Joseph has been gone from home for more than a decade at this point. This thirty-year-old Joseph who stands before Pharaoh is a very different Joseph from the seventeen-year-old dreamer in Genesis 37. Joseph now exhibits significant spiritual maturity. Pits and prisons will accomplish that for those who keep their eyes on God. Spiritual maturity is always marked by exhibiting humility, practicing gentleness, and giving God all the glory. The man facing Pharaoh beautifully reflects all of this.

What events in your life have made a significant impact on your spiritual maturity?

If the events in your life are anything like mine, they have not always been pleasant. But as steel is forged in the fire, so is spiritual maturity.

JOSEPH'S INTERPRETATION AND RECOMMENDATIONS
Read Genesis 41:17–36.

God uses Joseph to accurately interpret the dreams He gave Pharoah and prudently goes a step further to recommend emergency courses of action to avoid the worst-case scenario for Egypt.

Nowhere in Joseph's interpretation or recommendation does he ever hint that such wisdom comes from within.

How do you see this in Genesis 41:28 and 41:32?

Joseph makes it plain to Pharaoh and his entire court that when God speaks, mountains will be moved.

In Genesis 41:33–34, what three specific action items does Joseph suggest to Pharaoh?

1.

2.

3.

Appoint a main man, appoint overseers under him, and gather one-fifth of Egypt's produce. Each task is as important as the next to preserve the people through the coming famine. In God's goodness, He will send the plenty before He sends the famine. God gives time to prepare provisions from one season to the next. What a beautiful glimpse of God's grace to those Egyptians!

God extends that same grace in our lives. At fifty-five years old, I have learned firsthand to be as frugal in times of plenty as in times of want, for one always follows the other throughout life.

How have you seen this truth in your own life?

As we close today's lesson, we remember that God has given us priceless plenty in bread that will never grow stale or run out.

Write out John 6:27.

Time spent gathering and preserving is vital because there will come a time of spending.

Jesus is our bread that never perishes but endures to everlasting life. And whatever hardships or difficult seasons we must endure, the labor is worth it.

Go Quiet, Go Deep

Quiet your mind from distractions and pull your Bible close. Bow your head and ask Jesus to make His Word and today's lesson personal for you.

Take your time writing out Proverbs 2:5.

What does it mean to you personally to understand the fear of the Lord and find the knowledge of God?

I pray that the boundless love, grace, and forgiveness of Jesus would penetrate every barrier today so that He can work in you and through you.

DAY 3

JOSEPH'S RISE TO POWER

And Pharaoh said to his servants, "Can we find a man like this, in whom is the Spirit of God?" Then Pharaoh said to Joseph, "Since God has shown you all this, there is none so discerning and wise as you are. You shall be over my house, and all my people shall order themselves as you command. Only as regards the throne will I be greater than you." (Genesis 41:38–40)

Today's lesson reveals a monumental life change for Joseph on every level. Upon hearing that Joseph could accurately interpret dreams, Pharaoh released Joseph from prison. Joseph not only interpreted Pharaoh's troubling dreams but he also provided solid action points for Pharaoh to consider to avoid devastation during the foreseen famine.

A dear pastor friend (who has long since retired) held to a wise saying during his active ministry years: "If you approach me with a problem, be ready to provide three ways we can solve it." This mindset not only created unity and a sense of common purpose but also inspired God's people to utilize their God-given gifts. I have never forgotten his incredibly wise advice. Joseph did exactly the same thing for Pharaoh.

Read Genesis 41:37–41. What stands out to you in these verses?

JOSEPH'S WITNESS

There is nothing in the text that even hints that Joseph was putting himself forward for the position. He simply listened to God, interpreted Pharaoh's dreams, and offered three solid action points to work toward.

What does Pharaoh say in Genesis 41:38?

And at that moment, a pagan Pharaoh glimpsed the living God. Did you notice that Pharaoh did not say those words to Joseph? He marveled aloud to his servants, perhaps as if to say, "Do you see what I see in this man?" To see God through a man's work and words is infinitely valuable.

Whether you work inside or outside the home, work is an important part of our lives. What do the following verses reveal about work?

2 Thessalonians 3:10–12

Colossians 3:23–24

Genesis 2:15

How do those verses clarify for you how we are to work?

Whether you are up early to pack lunches for your kids, sit at a computer in a cubicle, or scrub bathrooms, your diligent work gives glory to God. But there is an important aspect of work that most in our culture today completely ignore.

Write out Exodus 20:8–10.

God created work; He also created rest. Embracing both in equal measure leads to an enriching, balanced spiritual life. Someone who boasts about working eighty-hour weeks may believe they have mastered work—but actually, they have become its slave. Work, rather than God, has become their identity.

If you struggle with work and rest balance, pause here. Ask God to rearrange your priorities to embrace rest alongside your work.

EGYPT'S NEW PRIME MINISTER
Read Genesis 41:42–45.

Fewer than twenty-four hours before, Joseph was a prisoner wearing prison garb with no hint that his circumstances would change for the better. Now he stands before Pharaoh as the prime minister of Egypt, wearing Pharaoh's signet ring, sporting fine clothes, and being assigned to ride in the chariot immediately behind Pharaoh. What an incredible example of God's will coming to fruition for Joseph and for His people!

As an aside, can you imagine the scene in Potiphar's home that morning? I can almost picture the *Egyptian Gazette* arriving at his front door while he lingered over morning coffee with his wife. He picks up the paper, brings it in, and starts reading portions aloud. Can you imagine the reaction of Potiphar's wife as she learns the identity of Egypt's new prime minister? I wonder if she and her husband suddenly felt the urge to go on holiday.

But back to the story. There is an interesting parallel to Joseph's situation in the life of Daniel. After he was released from the lions' den, Daniel was raised to the chief magistrate at the right hand of Darius, ruling all the Persian Empire (see Daniel 6:1–28).

Even small changes can deeply affect our lives. However, Joseph experienced significant changes in every area of his life.

Have you ever stepped into a position in life, whether work, family situation, or in church, where it completely changed how your future would look? If so, how did you process the change?

Joseph not only stepped into a new work role but he was also given a new name and a new bride.

According to Genesis 41:45, what name did Pharaoh give Joseph?

The name Pharaoh bestowed on Joseph not only demonstrated Pharaoh's authority over Joseph but also reflected the value that Pharaoh saw in Joseph. The name *Zaphenath-paneah* likely means "revealer of secrets." Most appropriate, given the circumstances of their meeting. The verse also reveals that Pharaoh gave Joseph a bride.

Who was Joseph's bride, and whose daughter was she?

At first glance, we may be confused that Asenath was the daughter of the same Potiphar who already appeared in Joseph's narrative. But this Asenath's father was Potiphera, the priest of On.

The remains of the Egyptian city of On (later called Heliopolis) are located approximately ten miles northeast of modern-day Cairo. Although its history is obscure, archaeologists have determined from ancient records that it was important as both a capital city and religious sanctuary for worshipers of the sun god Ra.[7]

In the span of a few moments, Joseph is given a new job with extraordinary responsibility, a new name, and a new wife. Pharaoh has exalted Joseph above all in Egypt, apart from himself.

EXALTED ABOVE ALL

Here again, we find a parallel between Joseph and Jesus. Joseph had suffered greatly yet humbled himself before Pharaoh. Joseph was eventually raised to the right hand of Pharaoh to rule all of Egypt.

What does Philippians 2:8–10 tell us about Jesus?

After Jesus suffered and was buried, He was raised and ascended to the right hand of the Father to rule all of creation. Just as Joseph was raised to Pharaoh's right hand but given a chariot to go throughout Egypt to carry out his rule, Jesus is not sitting someplace in heaven far away from us—He is with us always, filling His whole creation. In Jesus, we have the ultimate revealer of secrets (see John 1:17–18).

In the exaltation of Christ, you and I have a Savior who holds all power over heaven and earth. He is the grace-dispenser, chief ruler of God among men, and the lover of our souls.

No matter what pits or prisons this life throws us into, Jesus never leaves our side and will one day exalt us to live with Him for all eternity. Now that, friends, is a beautiful change we never need to dread or fear. Praise God!

Go Quiet, Go Deep

Quiet your mind from distractions and pull your Bible close. Bow your head and ask Jesus to make His Word and today's lesson personal for you.

Take your time writing out 1 Corinthians 10:31.

What does it mean to you personally that your work is to be done for the glory of God?

I pray that the boundless love, grace, and forgiveness of Jesus would penetrate every barrier today so that He can work in you and through you.

DAY 4

PLENTIFUL GATHERING

> Joseph was thirty years old when he entered the service of Pharaoh king of Egypt. And Joseph went out from the presence of Pharaoh and went through all the land of Egypt. (Genesis 41:46)

Thirteen years after Joseph's brothers had thrown him into a waterless pit and sold him to Midianite traders, Joseph now humbly steps up onto the largest stage of his life. From the time he was a teenager (and likely even before then), God had prepared Joseph for this. And he was ready.

Here we see how God, in His perfect timing and wisdom, had systematically prepared Joseph throughout many hard years to hone his administrative gifts in Potiphar's house and in prison. God removed jealous brothers, distractions, and even his worldly freedom so Joseph would know beyond any shadow of a doubt that God alone was the one who brought it about.

Like a master chess player, God moved people, events, and hearts to place Joseph in precisely the right place with the power and authority to save not only His people but all of Egypt.

Read Genesis 41:46–49. What stands out to you in these verses?

Joseph rises in power to the place God prepared for him—he settles down, begins a family, and gets to work managing Egypt's resources to save the people from famine. And during all of this, Pharoah saw in Joseph the God of Abraham, Isaac, and Jacob.

SEVEN YEARS OF PLENTY

Joseph immediately puts God's plan into action to gather and store Egypt's great harvests. He did not have the attitude that they had "plenty of time." He diligently worked and traveled throughout Egypt as if the famine would begin the next day.

I believe Joseph's diligence stands in stark contrast to our culture today. Countless studies have shown how Americans are terrible at saving yet excel at spending. In a similar crisis, it is not hard to imagine how many Americans would take the approach of there is "plenty of time" before the worst happens.

Now apply that concept to our faith lives. We know that literally billions of people have not heard about nor received God's gift of faith for eternal salvation. What do the following verses say about the time we have?

1 Corinthians 7:29–31

1 Peter 4:7

2 Peter 3:10

As a recovering procrastinator and glass-half-full person, I tend to put on rose-colored glasses that fool me into believing there is *plenty* of time. Plenty of time to have that important conversation with a family member who does not know Jesus as Lord and Savior. Plenty of time to _____. How would you fill in that blank?

The startling truth is that we don't know if the Lord will return tomorrow, next month, or one thousand years from now. He urges us to live intentionally and share His Gospel diligently without hesitation or delay.

Pause here to think of your daily routine. Who do you regularly come in contact with but do not know if they know Jesus? How could you start a conversation? Ask the Lord for His perfect timing to guide your words.

Joseph Welcomes Two Sons

Read Genesis 41:50–52.

God blesses Joseph and his wife with two sons: Manasseh and Ephraim. They would eventually become the heads of two tribes of Israel. Out of Jacob's twelve sons, only Joseph was not appointed as head of one of the tribes of Israel. Instead, his two sons were each given their own tribe, which, combined, comprised the twelfth tribe. In this, God gave Joseph a double blessing. Some scholars even refer to Manasseh and Ephraim as the two half-tribes of Joseph.

Manasseh

According to Genesis 41:51, why did Joseph name his firstborn *Manasseh*?

Over the years, I have heard countless women give their reasons for having more than one child. One reason often rises head and shoulders above the rest: the pain and suffering they endured during childbirth was nothing compared to the blessing of the children they welcomed.

Here, Joseph offers a similar reason. As he looks back on his suffering—in the pit, as a slave, and then as a prisoner—perhaps Joseph concludes that the blessing of being Egypt's prime minister in a prosperous land with a beautiful family far outweighs the pain. Joseph looks in the rearview mirror to see the trail of God's faithfulness and realizes just how blessed he has been.

Manasseh's name also meant that Joseph forgot all his father's house. The reference here is not that he forgot the people but rather that he forgot the jealous unkindness he received from his older brothers. Perhaps it also includes his father's favoritism, which caused their sibling rift in the first place.

Joseph demonstrates one of the most powerful and beautiful acts of forgiveness in all of Scripture. Joseph could have allowed anger and bitterness to swallow his life whole and destroy him completely. We have seen people like that. Maybe we have been that person. Instead, Joseph looked up and trusted God. Then he names his firstborn son in such a way as to never forget God's loving faithfulness.

What does Colossians 3:13 say about forgiveness?

Forgiveness is such a vital part of our faith that it is literally commanded by God. Reconciliation is encouraged, but forgiveness is commanded.

I wrote an entire book about forgiveness, born out of a deep betrayal I experienced that placed me at a crossroads—much like Joseph. I had a choice: (1) I could allow hate and unforgiveness to destroy me and all those I loved, or (2) I could trust God to work forgiveness in my heart. That God-given forgiveness, both received and extended, has been one of the greatest blessings in my life.

EPHRAIM

According to Genesis 41:52, why did Joseph name his second-born son *Ephraim*?

If you have ever lost everything, you may have struggled with feeling that your life would never be fruitful again. I can certainly relate. Joseph was a favored son in a prominent household and wore an exquisite robe that garnered his brothers' enmity. He led a privileged life, indeed. Then, one day, his brothers' jealous rage changed Joseph's life forever. Perhaps you can relate to Joseph.

Have the pits and prisons in your life changed your outlook on life? If so, how?

If you are enduring a season of hardship, can you see your life being fruitful again one day? Why or why not?

One commentator explained a believer's dark seasons like this: "Light is sometimes sown for the righteous in a barren and unlikely soil; and yet if God sows it, and waters it, it will come up again. The afflictions of the saints promote their fruitfulness."[8]

What do the following verses say about light and darkness?

John 1:5

John 8:12

Ephesians 5:8

Jesus told His disciples (and us) that we will have trouble in this world. Period. But He has overcome the world! (See John 16:33.)

FRUITFUL DESPITE AFFLICTION

In Genesis 41:52, Joseph makes a significant reference that cannot be overlooked. He acknowledges that God has made him fruitful in the land of his affliction. *In* the land. Not rescued from the land. God did not rescue Joseph from prison but walked by him through it. Sometimes, God will remove us out of hurtful situations; other times, He allows them to play out and walks with us *through* them.

Have you found this true in your life? If so, what was the outcome?

Like Joseph, you and I will walk through seasons of plenty and famine. Where and on whom we place our focus makes all the difference. And in

God's perfect timing, one day He will usher us into our heavenly promised land—secured by Christ's blood on the cross.

Go Quiet, Go Deep

Quiet your mind from distractions and pull your Bible close. Bow your head and ask Jesus to make His Word and today's lesson personal for you.

Take your time writing out Psalm 30:5.

What does it mean to you personally that because of Jesus, your suffering is only temporary?

I pray that the boundless love, grace, and forgiveness of Jesus would penetrate every barrier today so that He can work in you and through you.

DAY 5

PERSEVERING IN HARDSHIP

The seven years of plenty that occurred in the land of Egypt came to an end, and the seven years of famine began to come, as Joseph had said. There was famine in all lands, but in all the land of Egypt there was bread. (Genesis 41:53–54)

Summers in south Texas can be brutal. Extreme heat and lack of rain can quickly drain water stores and shut down power grids.

Spiritually speaking, seasons of abundance can be both a blessing and a danger. Through His gifts of provision, the Lord blesses us with renewed hope, peace, and a sense of well-being. Those abundant seasons open our clenched fists to more readily help one another and His mission work. They unfold opportunities for us to think past our normal routine to embrace dreams and new possibilities. Abundant seasons are incredible blessings from God.

Seasons of blessing can also pose spiritual dangers. How many of us seek the Lord and His guidance diligently when all is well? If we are not careful, those abundant seasons can cause spiritual atrophy. Perhaps our prayer muscles are not exercised as much. Maybe our zeal to seek His guidance wanes as we lapse into a spiritual coma of self-indulgences. It is tempting to spend more than we save because the well keeps filling with more blessings.

But then there are those seasons of famine. Suddenly, the well does not keep refilling. We stop short and begin taking stock of resources. Perhaps regret for frivolous pursuits seeps in. Our fists may start to clench again, and we find ourselves at the Lord's feet, asking what went wrong. Thankfully, Scripture provides clear examples of how to best navigate both seasons of abundance and seasons of famine.

SEASONS OF FAMINE
Read Genesis 41:53–55. What stands out to you in these verses?

Joseph never forgot God's interpretation of Pharaoh's dreams: "There will be seven years of great plenty . . . but after them there will arise seven years of famine" (Genesis 41:29–30). Joseph kept his eye on the ball. Even though he was surrounded by plenty, he never forgot that famine was coming.

We all experience seasons of famine—not necessarily a locust pestilence but perhaps hard seasons initiated by job loss, a serious health issue, or relationship rifts.

I experienced a spiritual famine when my dad died following a lengthy battle with cancer. I was a daddy's girl and had never prayed so hard. *God, just make him better.* And when God did not deliver, my self-imposed spiritual famine was immediate and severe.

My prayer life went to zero, and I was angry. *Really angry.* I stubbornly remained in that desert for more than two years, willfully shutting off the faucet of God's living water. Then one day, I just couldn't take another step in the dust. I cried out to God, and He opened the floodgates of forgiveness, love, and comfort that only He can give.

That is a very hard season for me to look back on. Yet I learned lessons in that desert that I would not have learned otherwise. And even though I am thankful for that season today, I never want to experience such spiritual dehydration again.

What was your last season of spiritual famine?

How did you navigate it?

Having walked through such a season, I learned five indicators of spiritual dehydration. I pray that these are helpful if you are struggling through such a season today.

1. *Coarse talk.* If you have ever experienced physical dehydration, you know that it causes bad breath. The words you speak provide clear indicators of your spiritual health.

What does Luke 6:45 say?

2. *Fatigue.* Perhaps you have become a social hermit, not wanting to leave the house or even your bed. Being spiritually drained results in no overflow to pour into the lives of others, so you don't bother trying.

What does Philippians 1:9–11 say?

3. *Anger.* You have no bandwidth to temper your words, so your kindness filter takes a vacation. Before you know it, you have a quick temper and a sharp tongue.

What does James 3:8–10 say?

4. *The presence of sin.* Since you have temporarily ignored the Spirit's control over your life, your flesh takes over and you develop a lack of self-control. That could manifest itself in various addictive and destructive behaviors.

What does Galatians 5:23 say?

5. *Poor decision-making.* This goes hand in hand with the point above. You start downplaying sin and begin to make unwise choices. Such foolishness can have serious consequences.

What does Proverbs 18:1–3 say?

I experienced all five of these during that spiritual famine. If you are exhibiting any of these signs of spiritual dehydration, pause right now. You will not survive a spiritual famine apart from the Lord's guidance and provision.

If you are angry, then yell. If you are overcome, then cry. And when you are finished, bow your head before the Lord and ask for His forgiveness. He has never left your side. Give Him access to your heart, mind, and soul once again. He will hydrate you with His living water.

Due to Joseph's hard work and tenacity to follow the Lord, all the land of Egypt had bread. If any Egyptian had complained about how much grain and produce Joseph had gathered the seven years before, it is safe to assume that any complaining ceased instantaneously.

JOSEPH'S DILIGENCE
Read Genesis 41:55–57. What stands out to you in these verses?

The famine did not just affect Egypt but "all the earth." Joseph had taken the Lord's instructions to heart so faithfully that not only did all of Egypt have food but there was enough to supply envoys from all the earth.

When people approach Pharaoh for bread, what did he instruct in Genesis 41:55?

If Pharaoh had not recognized it before, he is now fully aware of Joseph's value as a leader and administrator. Events transpired just as Joseph interpreted. Pharaoh sees because God faithfully worked through Joseph, Egypt not only survived but prospered. Had Egypt been destroyed by the famine, Pharaoh would have been king over scorpions and sand instead of people.

In a sense, Pharaoh owed his job to Joseph's diligence. He was still king, but when people approached him for bread, Pharaoh directed the people to the supply source. Likewise, God directs you and me to our only source of mercy, grace, and forgiveness. Write out the following verses:

1 Chronicles 22:19a

Isaiah 55:6

God is the only true source for everything we need—physically, mentally, emotionally, and spiritually. We can trust in His perfect timing.

Just as God enabled Joseph to stand firm in Him during times of plenty and famine, God gives us His strength to do likewise.

God knows how much those famines hurt.

Inhale His promises deeply.

Exhale the pain completely.

One day at a time.

Jesus catches every tear.

Pray through your waiting.

And focus on your Savior, not on the sand.

Go Quiet, Go Deep

Quiet your mind from distractions and pull your Bible close. Bow your head and ask Jesus to make His Word and today's lesson personal for you.

Take your time writing out Jeremiah 29:13.

What does it mean to you personally that when you seek God with all your heart, you will find Him?

I pray that the boundless love, grace, and forgiveness of Jesus would penetrate every barrier today so that He can work in you and through you.

WEEK 4

FEAST AND FAMINE

Genesis 42–43

In the middle of hardship and in the grip of severe famine, Joseph's past comes walking through the front door. The devastating famine has reached Canaan and drives Joseph's brothers to Egypt for food.

For more than twenty years, Joseph's brothers successfully hid their cowardly, heartless act of selling Joseph into slavery. The day of reckoning has finally arrived.

DAY 1   Desperation Moves Us *(Genesis 42:1–5)*

DAY 2   Revenge or Second Chance? *(Genesis 42:6–17)*

DAY 3   The Lessons of Past Sins *(Genesis 42:18–38)*

DAY 4   Returning Again *(Genesis 43:1–15)*

DAY 5   Invited to the Table *(Genesis 43:16–34)*

KEY QUESTIONS:

- What process has God used in your life to uncover sin, whether old or new?

- What did you learn throughout the process?

- In those instances, did someone's words or actions ignite the process?

DAY 1

DESPERATION MOVES US

When Jacob learned that there was grain for sale in Egypt, he said to his sons, "Why do you look at one another?" And he said, "Behold, I have heard that there is grain for sale in Egypt. Go down and buy grain for us there, that we may live and not die." (Genesis 42:1–2)

Up to this point, we have seen how the dreams Joseph interpreted for the chief cupbearer, chief baker, and Pharaoh have been fulfilled. Now we will see how God fulfilled the dreams Joseph shared with his brothers before his life was completely upended.

Joseph's narrative now focuses on what transpired between Joseph and his brothers as Jacob's ten older sons travel to Egypt to secure food for their families. The story is both entertaining and instructive. However, it all points to one overarching goal: to remove Jacob's family from Canaan. Eventually, God would work some of the greatest miracles in Scripture to rescue His children from bondage.

Read Genesis 42:1–5. What stands out to you in these verses?

Personally, I love Jacob's no-nonsense approach to the crisis. In modern terms, as he sees his sons just blinking at one another, he tells them, "Don't sit there like lumps on a log; *do* something!" I am smiling because I can hear my parents' voices in the text. I mean, what parent has not, at one point or another, told their children to get a move on?

FAMINE IN CANAAN

The famine across the land had broken through the boundaries of Egypt and began affecting the surrounding lands, including Canaan. When we look throughout Scripture, famines were not an unusual occurrence for Israel's patriarchs. In the following verses, who experienced a famine?

Genesis 12:10

Genesis 26:1–5

Did you notice that during Isaac's time of famine, God instructed Isaac *not* to go to Egypt? Rather, after Abraham's death, God moved Isaac from Beer-lahai-roi (see Genesis 25:11) to the Valley of Gerar (see Genesis 26:17). Archaeologists have determined that Gerar bordered the Promised Land.

During Isaac's lifetime, God moved His people *toward* the Promised Land to establish their inheritance there forever. Yet against God's command, they began to intermarry with pagan nations (see Genesis 26:34–35). Consequently, during Jacob's famine (the famine of this study), God moved his people *away* from the Promised Land and pagan temptations in order to preserve them in the lush land of Goshen in Egypt.

Sometimes when you and I become entrenched in worldly culture, God intervenes to wean us from worldly pursuits that lure our attention away from Him and His purposes.

What does Hebrews 11:14–16 tell us?

The "homeland" referred to in verse 14 literally means the "fatherland" (heaven).[9] As God weans us from the things of this world, He stirs in us a longing to seek Him and His homeland.

Recall a time over the years when God intervened in your life to move your attention away from worldly pursuits.

What circumstance or thought pattern did He remove you from?

Did you fight the move? If so, how?

What did He accomplish in your life as a result?

As you look back, how did you grow spiritually from that experience?

God never moves us (geographically or otherwise) simply for the sake of moving us. Much like famines, God's purpose is never to enjoy watching our suffering but to bring us to a place where we seek Him and long for His provision in our lives.

FAMINES IN THE ANCIENT WORLD

Whether from warfare, invaders, or natural causes, famines directly affected both agriculture and livestock (see Joel 1, Isaiah 7). Consequently, famine directly affected people and their very survival. It was not uncommon for people to operate as if they were only a step ahead of starvation.

Scholars have widely held that homestead farming was common in the ancient world. Families and communities embraced homestead (subsistence) farming to provide most, if not all, of the food and goods they needed, as well as surplus to sell for income.

As a fairly new sustainable gardener, I totally understand that ancient world mindset. As America has experienced the price of food, gas, and goods soaring due to inflation, I have gravitated to growing many of my own vegetables and some fruit over the past few years. Along the way, God has given me the additional blessing of truly loving gardening and the time I spend with Him meditating on His Word and His promises in that beautiful, peaceful place.

And in both the ancient world and even today, food shortages can be easily exacerbated by hoarding. Remember the toilet paper dilemma during the pandemic?

Sometimes during those ancient world famines, God literally stopped the rain for years at a time. There is not much you can do as a gardener or

Meant for Good

farmer if there is no water for livestock, fields, or gardens.

Again, God never brought on such hardship to simply watch His people squirm. It was an exercise to bring the people to the end of their own dependence and to again depend on God alone as their provider. Today, He still works in our lives to bring us to the point to trusting Him in all things and for all things. We are safe in His hands!

Jacob Playing Favorites, Again

Even though Jacob's sons were grown, married, and had responsibilities of their own, Jacob ordered them to go to Egypt. In a patriarchal society, such commands were followed as if they were law. In fact, the task was so important that rather than send servants, Jacob sent his sons.

His sons were merely standing around looking at one another. Perhaps they were deliberating and debating what should be done. Perhaps they had also heard about the grain but were playing "rock, paper, scissors" to determine who would make the journey to Egypt. Scripture is silent as to their reasons for inactivity.

You and I can probably agree that spending time formulating plans is wise and prudent. However, at some point, we all have to step out and get moving. Unlike Scarlett O'Hara, we cannot always just think about things tomorrow. Some things cannot wait that long.

What does Genesis 42:4 reveal?

Sigh. Jacob has apparently not yet learned the collateral damage caused by playing favorites among his children. Granted, Jacob did not know the true story behind Joseph's disappearance. But with Joseph gone, Jacob now clings to Benjamin as his beloved Rachel's only remaining son. Old habits are hard to break, aren't they?

Sometimes destructive habits or tendencies keep cropping up in our lives, even though we are fully aware of how harmful they can be.

Do you have such a habit or tendency?

If so, what is it and what dangers have you identified that could result from it?

What step could you take today to initiate a change in that behavior?

Without a doubt, my destructive behavior is unhealthy eating habits. I have struggled with being overweight my entire adult life. Although I have no resulting health issues from bad eating habits yet, I realize that health challenges *will* surface if I don't change. Because entrenched habits like mine are very hard to break, I have to rely on God to strengthen my will to change and be a good steward of the body He provided me. Diving deep into complicated habits and eating issues would fill an entire book. God willing, He will one day inspire those permanent changes in my life and motivate me to actually write that book and help others make the same changes.

As Jacob displays favoritism toward Benjamin, it makes us wonder if the older brothers had become as harsh and jealous toward Benjamin as they had been toward Joseph. Or perhaps lingering guilt about how they treated Joseph caused them to be nicer to their youngest brother. Since Scripture is silent, we can only speculate regarding the health of their sibling relationship.

As we close today's lesson, the famine in Joseph's narrative rages through Canaan. And at Jacob's command, the older brothers pack up and steer their camels toward Egypt.

The famine of unrepentant sin also rages within the brothers. The shame of selling Joseph and lying to their father resides in their hearts. Little do they know that God is bringing the sons of Israel to Egypt to begin eradicating both sin and shame through His grace and forgiveness.

When you and I look to God and trust Him for strength and guidance, we can be assured that a famine in our lives will not cause a famine in our hearts.

Go Quiet, Go Deep

Quiet your mind from distractions and pull your Bible close. Bow your head and ask Jesus to make His Word and today's lesson personal for you.

Take your time writing out 1 Corinthians 10:13.

What does it mean to you personally that God has provided an escape hatch for every temptation and destructive behavior that you experience?

I pray that the boundless love, grace, and forgiveness of Jesus would penetrate every barrier today so that He can work in you and through you.

DAY 2

REVENGE OR SECOND CHANCE?

Now Joseph was governor over the land. He was the one who sold to all the people of the land. And Joseph's brothers came and bowed themselves before him with their faces to the ground. Joseph saw his brothers and recognized them, but he treated them like strangers and spoke roughly to them. "Where do you come from?" he said. They said, "From the land of Canaan, to buy food." And Joseph recognized his brothers, but they did not recognize him. (Genesis 42:6–8)

Martin Luther made this observation: you must know God as an enemy before you can know Him as a friend.[10] Uncovering sin is never a pleasant process, but it is a necessary one for God to restore us to Him and to one another. We need to be reminded that sin separates us from God. And that is a dark, lonely, scary place, indeed. Only by the blood of the Lamb is that separation repaired.

The sin of Joseph's brothers had caused grief, heartache, and separation. God now begins the restoration process, but it gets ugly before it gets better.

Read Genesis 42:6–8. What stands out to you in these verses?

As the ten older brothers arrive in Egypt to obtain food for their families, they have no clue they are fulfilling the dream they had loathed. Suddenly, they are facedown before the brother that they had so horribly mistreated—and they do not recognize him. After all, more than twenty years have passed. Joseph dresses, talks, and acts like an Egyptian. He even uses an interpreter so his brothers will not recognize his voice (see Genesis 42:23).

Joseph, however, recognizes his brothers immediately. It makes us wonder if he ever thought this moment would happen. If he ever realized how far the famine would spread. Yet Joseph had set aside that old grudge long ago and let it be replaced with the healing balm of forgiveness. Or had he?

Unforgiveness or Just Busy?

Joseph was in a powerful position with command over Pharaoh's armies. Why did he never send a chariot to let his father know that his favorite son was still alive? Although Joseph "went through all the land of Egypt" (Genesis 41:46), he never quite made it to Canaan where his family lived. Did Joseph struggle with unforgiveness?

When we have been hurt, sometimes it is easier to mouth the words of forgiveness than to actually walk toward it. We may say that we forgive the person who hurt us, but do we find ourselves conveniently unavailable when they come around?

Is there someone in your life whom you struggle to forgive? If so, who is it and what happened?

How long ago was that hurt initiated?

Do you believe that by God's power you have truly forgiven that person?

One question I am asked almost more than any other is this: How can I tell if I have truly forgiven someone? It comes down to this: If you are more sad about *who they have become* than *what they have done,* then God has truly worked forgiveness in your heart. If you are still uncertain whether you have actually extended forgiveness, here are four litmus tests:

1. *General Thoughts Test.* Can you think positive thoughts about this person? You've likely been in a close enough relationship with him or her to suffer such injury. Is there anything good about this person you can come up with? *If not, continue asking God to work forgiveness in you.*

2. *Failure Test.* When someone injures you, you can often wish harm upon him or her. Have you stopped looking for this person to fail? Forgiveness here means you would like this person to succeed or at least do better in life. *If not, continue asking God to work forgiveness in you.*

3. *Revenge Test.* Do you still dream about ways to get even with this person? . . . Do you still desire to somehow make them pay [physically, emotionally, or mentally] for hurting you? *If so, continue asking God to work forgiveness in you.*

4. *Opportunity to Help Test.* Would you help this person if you knew he or she were in trouble and you had the means and ability? I'm not suggesting that you subject yourself to further abuse or harm, but would you want this person to prosper or see him or her come to harm? *If harm, continue asking God to work forgiveness in you.*[11]

Did you pass? If not, which one(s) are you struggling with?

Take a moment to pause here and ask God to work forgiveness in your heart. By His grace and through His strength alone, one day, you will pass all four tests.

As the rest of the narrative will reveal, Joseph passes all four tests. There is no evidence on the pages of Scripture to suggest that Joseph harbored unforgiveness. He never reminds his brothers of their heinous actions or holds it over their heads for his advantage. He consistently looks to God for strength and, by example, points those around him to do likewise.

GOD BRINGS JOSEPH'S INITIAL DREAMS TO FRUITION
Read Genesis 42:9–14.

As the brothers' reunion unfolds, Joseph speaks harshly to them. But another startling thing happens: "Joseph remembered the dreams that he had dreamed of them."

In Genesis 37:7 and 37:9, what happened in Joseph's dreams?

Now, twenty years later, Joseph sees in real time that the dreams God gave him regarding his brothers had, in fact, been prophetic. Imagine how startling that moment was for Joseph. Can you imagine how many realizations may have struck Joseph instantaneously?

God saw today two decades ago.

God has been preparing me all along.

God was with me.

There was a reason for my suffering.

I am right where I am supposed to be.

What a beautiful display of God's grace in Joseph's life! Job springs to mind too. Job experienced severe loss and suffering and never knew why. In a split second, God gave Joseph what He never gave Job: *the reason for his suffering.* Suddenly, Joseph knew the *why* behind the *what.*

By the grace of God, when I recall hard seasons in my life to date, I can clearly see the handprints of God. He carried me in my weakness, comforted me in my sickness, and loved me through my brokenness. And when all was said and done, He gave me His strength to keep going so I can continue to honor the vocations He has given me and give Him all the glory.

Think back on your hard seasons. Where do you see His handprints?

God never promises to answer our *why.* He promises to faithfully walk with us through the *what.* He promises that His almighty presence goes with us through the dark times to usher us back into His glorious light. Grace upon grace!

Joseph's Harshness and Accusations

Read Genesis 42:9–17.

As the brothers' reunion unfolds, Joseph speaks harshly to them through the interpreter and even goes so far as to call them spies.

How does Joseph decide to test his brothers?

I would venture a guess that few things bring about honesty faster than being thrown into prison. Imagine the worries racing through the brothers' minds. They had been sent by their father to retrieve food from Egypt so their family would not perish from the famine. Their wives and children were still depending on them for survival. Every day counted.

Yet they were captive in prison. And as we look back on their actions toward a seventeen-year-old Joseph, we see that God began preparing that prison for them long before they arrived.

Not for their destruction but to bring about His good purposes.

Today, if you find yourself in a prison (emotionally, mentally, or spiritually), I pray that you can take hope and comfort from the fact that God's good purposes are always working in your life toward freedom in Christ.

Go Quiet, Go Deep

Quiet your mind from distractions and pull your Bible close. Bow your head and ask Jesus to make His Word and today's lesson personal for you.

Take your time writing out Colossians 3:13.

What does it mean to you personally that God does not just suggest forgiveness but rather commands it?

I pray that the boundless love, grace, and forgiveness of Jesus would penetrate every barrier today so that He can work in you and through you.

DAY 3

THE LESSONS OF PAST SINS

On the third day Joseph said to them, "Do this and you will live, for I fear God: if you are honest men, let one of your brothers remain confined where you are in custody, and let the rest go and carry grain for the famine of your households, and bring your youngest brother to me. So your words will be verified, and you shall not die." And they did so. (Genesis 42:18–20)

After leaving his ten older brothers in prison to stew in their thoughts for three days, Joseph releases them. However, he has a specific plan in mind. He longs to know if his only full-blooded brother, Benjamin, is alive and well. Let the games begin!

Read Genesis 42:18–20. What stands out to you in these verses?

RELEASED FROM PRISON

In the very first sentence Joseph speaks to his brothers upon their release, he gives them a surprising spiritual insight about himself that the brothers completely miss.

What does Joseph reveal about himself at the end of Genesis 42:18?

Joseph fears God. The Hebrew word Joseph chooses is *Elohim* (מִיהֹלֱא)— the one true God. Not an Egyptian god, not a general god, but the God of Abraham, Isaac, and his father Jacob. Perhaps the brothers were so overjoyed at their liberation from prison that they did not even pay attention to Joseph's choice of word to describe God. However, it shines a ray of hope into their situation.

JOSEPH DEMANDS TO SEE BENJAMIN

Joseph notices that his younger brother, Benjamin, is not among them. You can almost hear Joseph asking the unspoken question: "Did you sell my little brother as well?" That is why he declares that one of the brothers remain incarcerated while the other nine return to Canaan with supplies for their families. They are to retrieve Benjamin and return—or never return at all.

Did you notice that their word is not sufficient? Joseph slips in the phrase "If you are honest men" (v.19). Perhaps when Joseph was still at home, he took his older brothers' words at face value. Mistreatment often leads us to need physical proof if someone's words or character have come into question. Joseph tells his brothers that *only seeing his youngest brother* will save them from death.

If you have been hurt by someone in the past, what proof have you needed in order to trust him or her again?

How long did it take for you to trust that person again—or did you?

Often, the deeper the hurt, the longer it takes to reestablish trust. In cases of abuse, God does not require us to blindly trust that person—especially if there is a risk of future physical, mental, or spiritual harm. Trust is earned, not given.

GUILTY FEELINGS SURFACE
Read Genesis 42:21–23.

Upon their release, Joseph does not officially charge his brothers with any crime, accuse them of wrongdoing, or even mention who he is.

Yet what conclusion do the brothers reach in verse 21?

Guilt carries so much baggage. Psychologists describe it as a self-conscious emotion because it involves self-reflection. Like shame, pride, or embarrassment, guilt acts like a mirror. It's all about us. At that moment, the brothers see the true ugliness of their actions against Joseph twenty years earlier. God causes their unconfessed and unrepentant sin to roar to the surface in an instant.

If you are carrying around guilt over a sin that you have already (and perhaps repeatedly) repented to God, please hear this clearly: *He has forgiven you, according to His promises.* When we continue to feel guilt over our sin, God points us to Jesus' cross where that sin and guilt were paid in full: "It is finished" (John 19:30). Through Christ, every single sin was paid for on the cross. His blood has removed your guilt. Write out and soak in the following truths:

1 John 1:9

Psalm 85:2

Romans 8:1

Those are life-restoring words: *forgiven, cleansed,* and *not condemned.* The devil will always point us back to our sin in an attempt to debilitate us through guilt. Jesus points us to the cross to enable us to fully embrace the hope and future that we have through Him.

The brothers have no clue that Joseph can understand every word they are speaking to one another. Yet imagine the thoughts that may have run through Joseph's mind as their words hit deep. *They heard my distress. They heard me begging. Perhaps God has been working on them this whole time.*

How would you have reacted at that moment?

In the first sentence of Genesis 42:24, how did Joseph react?

We are not told that Joseph wept when his brothers threw him in a pit or sold him into slavery. Not when he lost his position in Potiphar's home and was thrown into prison. Not when the cupbearer and baker forgot him in prison. Not when he was released and honored by Pharoah. Not even when he got married or welcomed two sons. But for the first time in the narrative we are told here that Joseph wept.

Our greatest sorrows are not necessarily the result of *what* but of *who*. We will endure much hurt in this world, but if the perpetrator is family or someone we hold dear, that wound plunges deeper. Yet even there, God can bring healing. So Joseph wept privately (perhaps from grief over the years he and his family had lost or as an emotional release over forgiving his brothers). And God saw him and initiated the healing process in his life. Only God catches our every tear (see Psalm 56:8).

Read Genesis 42:24–25.

Joseph had a masterful way of letting the brothers realize the magnitude of what they had done without ever bringing it up himself. In fact, each time they talked about it after Joseph revealed himself to them throughout the rest of this story, he immediately turned the discussion to the good that God worked despite and through their sin.

The brothers perceived that the time had come to pay for their sin. They may have believed that their sin lay exposed for all to see. However, there is no indication that Pharaoh ever knew what Joseph's brothers had done, nor did anyone else at that point.

I believe this parallels what Jesus did with Judas at the Last Supper. Jesus found the perfect way to make Judas aware that He knew Judas was about to betray Him, without revealing or exposing him to the other disciples (see

John 13:26–28). Even when Judas left the Upper Room to carry out his foul deed, none of the remaining eleven were any the wiser about what he had gone to do (see John 13:21–25).

Throughout the Gospels, Jesus provided very few direct answers when people asked questions. He usually answered their question with a question or told a parable. When God brings about answers from within our own hearts and minds, the lessons learned stick with us much better than if an answer had been simply supplied.

How have you found this true in your own life?

This has certainly proven true on my spiritual journey. When external answers are supplied quickly, we miss out on that important faith-strengthening process of seeking after God in His Word and prayer to learn the answers.

THE TEST CONTINUES
Read Genesis 42:26–38.

After Joseph asks about the brothers' family situation, overhears them expressing remorse over past actions, and gives them needed supplies, we see the healing hope of God flicker in the darkness.

What do the brothers ask at the end of verse 28?

The brothers finally conclude that God is in the process of uncovering their sin: "What is this that God has done to us?" Those are sobering, instructive moments to say the very least. We know that God's purpose is to restore His children to Him through such uncovering, but even knowing that does not make it easier, does it?

After watching their brother Simeon bound and returned to prison, nine brothers return home with sacks of grain. They are completely unaware that the money they had paid for the grain had been returned to them. This is yet another aspect of Joseph's test to lead his brothers into fully acknowledging and repenting of their sin.

What is Jacob's response in Genesis 42:36?

After Jacob sees the sacks of money with the sacks of grain, he despairs. Perhaps he realizes that it was the second time that he had sent his older sons on a task, and they returned without one of their brothers.

Perhaps the times of famine and loss had taken their toll on Jacob because he only sees the bad scenario, not the life-saving grain. Even when Reuben offers to sacrifice his own two sons if the brothers fail to return with Benjamin, Jacob remains inconsolable.

Jacob struggles to see hope because his despair is not based on the facts.

Joseph is no more. But Joseph is not only alive, he is the prime minister of Egypt.

Simeon is no more. But Simeon is not only alive, he is in the safest place possible under the protective care of his brother, the prime minister.

Everything is against me. But since God is for us, no one can be against us.

As we look back on our hard seasons of life, we can certainly empathize with Jacob's despair. But is our despair based on fact or fiction?

When you and I struggle to see hope, sometimes we look around instead of looking up. We slip into walking by sight and not by faith. What do the following verses say about hope?

Psalm 62:5

Romans 15:4

Hebrews 10:23

As we close today's lesson, spend extra time reading and praying through the verses that you just wrote above.

Each day on earth is both a blessing and a battle.

Despite the severity of our battles, you and I can stand confident in Christ's victory over sin, death, and the grave.

No matter how deep we fall in life, God delights in lifting us back to Himself.

Go Quiet, Go Deep

Quiet your mind from distractions and pull your Bible close. Bow your head and ask Jesus to make His Word and today's lesson personal for you.

Take your time writing out Romans 8:1.

What does it mean to you personally that when you have sinned and guilt threatens to overwhelm you, Jesus does not condemn you?

I pray that the boundless love, grace, and forgiveness of Jesus would penetrate every barrier today so that He can work in you and through you.

DAY 4

RETURNING AGAIN

> Now the famine was severe in the land. And when they had eaten the grain that they had brought from Egypt, their father said to them, "Go again, buy us a little food." (Genesis 43:1–2)

As we open today's lesson, famine rages throughout the land of Egypt and beyond. As it becomes increasingly severe, Jacob's situation and that of his family again become desperate. They have consumed the initial provisions that the nine brothers had brought back from Egypt.

Today, again, we see the patriarch Jacob struggle with his faith. Faced with the potential loss of the last son of his beloved Rachel, Jacob has started to doubt the promises God made to him, his father, Isaac, and his grandfather Abraham. I don't know about you, but that has been hard for me to watch. Now Jacob again turns his thoughts and eyes back toward Egypt.

Read Genesis 43:1–6. What stands out to you in these verses?

THE DILEMMA

At last glance, Jacob was adamant that Benjamin not be taken to Egypt because losing him on top of losing Joseph would utterly destroy him. However, Jacob took that brave stance when he had received abundant provisions for his family. Taking a stand in times of plenty is one thing; taking a stand in times of poverty looks vastly different.

Have you taken a similar stand in the past? If so, what happened?

I believe many of us took hard stands of one kind or another during the pandemic. But as supplies grew thin, family and friends (or even ourselves) became ill, and many freedoms we took for granted (freedom to worship, among others) became curtailed, perhaps our bravado softened. With that in mind, perhaps we can relate a little better to Jacob's situation. *The famine in the land was severe.* He had no choice but to amend his stance.

Perhaps Jacob held on to the hope that by the time they would need more provisions, the famine would be over, and they could once again rely on their own storehouses. You can almost see Jacob's worry lines deepening as the famine worsens and supplies dwindle dangerously low once again.

So Jacob instructs his nine older sons to return to Egypt to purchase additional provisions. Judah moves center stage and reminds his father that Egypt's prime minister demanded Benjamin's presence in order to receive any more provisions.

What is Jacob's response in Genesis 43:6?

Jacob still grieves the decision that he knows must be made for the good of his whole family. Jacob is so relatable here!

How often have you delayed making a difficult decision because neither proposed option seemed good? If so, what happened?

In my early twenties, after I started working at my first law firm, I claimed way too many exemptions on my W-2. When tax time rolled around, instead of receiving a refund, I received a bill from the IRS for $1,200. *Ugh.* That may not seem like a lot in today's currency, but for a broke, single, twenty-four-year-old woman in the early nineties trying to make it in the big city, it was a lot.

The IRS offered two options: (1) I could pay off the total amount in one lump sum and wipe the slate clean immediately, or (2) I could pay it off in installments *plus* interest for the time delay. Well. I did not have $1,200. I was too proud to borrow money from my parents. So I went with the second option, grumbling about it the whole time.

My dilemma wasn't as dire as Jacob's, but I can relate to him. Perhaps you can too.

Judah Steps Up
Read Genesis 43:7–10.

Afterward, we can almost hear the brothers' exasperation as they jointly remind their father of the prime minister's *nonnegotiable* terms.

Then Judah speaks up again and offers to take all the heat if they will just get going.

Making the Wise Decision
Read Genesis 43:11–15.

As Jacob's sons prepare to return to Egypt, Jacob decides to send a gift to Egypt's prime minister to ease any hard feelings he may harbor toward his older sons for returning home the first time with both the grain *and* the money for the grain.

In Genesis 43:11–12, what items did Jacob command his sons to take?

Again, Jacob is so relatable here! In modern terms, Jacob wants to grease the palm of the prime minister to avoid possible retribution. This approach is not new in Jacob's life.

With the help of his mother, Rebecca, Jacob tricked his father, Isaac, to steal the blessing of his older brother, Esau. After spending twenty years apart, Jacob prepared to meet his brother.

What did Jacob take for Esau in Genesis 32:13–15?

Old habits die hard. Although it may seem that this gift to the man ruling Egypt is a paltry offering compared to what Jacob gave Esau years before, there is a severe famine now. The honey, nuts, and other items were likely harvested before the famine, which made them extraordinarily valuable. Those provisions had probably been keeping Jacob and his family alive when the grain ran out.

However, what made this offering truly remarkable is that Jacob included his youngest son, Benjamin. Not for the prime minister to keep, but to leverage him as a bargaining chip. Now, with the offering for Egypt's prime minister sorted out, Jacob tells his sons to retrieve more grain from Egypt.

What does Jacob finally conclude at the end of Genesis 43:14?

Jacob concludes that whatever will be, will be. As a music person, I can almost hear Doris Day singing "Que Sera, Sera" in the background. Although it may be hard to recognize at face value, Jacob's prayer is actually a powerful, faith-filled prayer.

Many people believe that a faith-filled prayer is one that claims only a good outcome and works in that belief. However, a true prayer of faith is one that trusts God *regardless* of the outcome.

The Book of Hebrews, also known as the "Hall of Faith," provides beautiful examples of many faith-filled believers. What did these people of faith pray during hard circumstances?

Noah in Hebrews 11:7

Abraham in Hebrews 11:8–10

Sarah in Hebrews 11:11

One particular faith-filled prayer in my life began in the summer of 2021 and is ongoing. On June 11, 2021, God moved me out of a law firm and into full-time ministry. He orchestrated obtaining 501(c)(3) nonprofit status for the ministry and provided an incredible, faith-filled Board of Directors as ministry partners and wise mentors around me.

For over a year and a half now, my heartfelt prayer has been for God to use every bit of time, energy, resources, and influence He provides me so I can write about Jesus, teach people about Him, and create resources to get people into God's Word.

I do not know how this ministry journey will turn out, or the bumps and blessings that await, but I know one thing beyond every shadow of a doubt: *I trust Jesus to lead the charge.* Period. And whatever will be, will be. Praise God!

What faith-filled prayer can you lift up to God today regarding your life, goals, or circumstances?

After Jacob determines that he will meet the prime minister's demands regardless of the outcome, he packs up a valuable gift and gives permission for his sons to go. With double the grain money in hand and Benjamin with them, the older brothers set off again for Egypt.

SACRIFICIAL OFFERING

There is one aspect of the passages we have covered today that we cannot miss: as Jacob struggles in his faith, he concludes that only one choice matters: Should he protect one son's life or surrender that son to save the rest? At that point, his son Judah steps up.

In Genesis 43:9, what pledge does Judah make to Jacob?

This is a beautiful picture of what Christ has done for us! In this account, both Jacob and Judah (Jesus' human ancestor) portray beautiful pictures of

Jesus. God could not fathom relegating His beloved children to hell for all eternity.

So, before the foundations of the earth were even formed, He orchestrated an escape hatch in the form of His one and only Son. Jesus died for the sins of all people and rose victorious over death, and all who believe that He is their Lord and Savior are forgiven and reconciled to God the Father through Him.

God does not want us separated from Him for a moment.

Much less for all of eternity.

He simply, profoundly, amazingly loves us too much.

Go Quiet, Go Deep

Quiet your mind from distractions and pull your Bible close. Bow your head and ask Jesus to make His Word and today's lesson personal for you.

Take your time writing out John 20:27.

What does it mean to you personally that when you, like Jacob, struggle in your faith, you can believe and trust in Jesus?

I pray that the boundless love, grace, and forgiveness of Jesus would penetrate every barrier today so that He can work in you and through you.

DAY 5

INVITED TO THE TABLE

When Joseph saw Benjamin with them, he said to the steward of his house, "Bring the men into the house, and slaughter an animal and make ready, for the men are to dine with me at noon." The man did as Joseph told him and brought the men to Joseph's house. (Genesis 43:16–17)

After receiving Jacob's blessing to return to Egypt for a second time to secure grain for their families, Joseph's brothers arrive and stand before him. This is the day Joseph has been hoping and waiting for. Benjamin is with them! And the test clock continues to tick.

Read Genesis 43:16–17. What stands out to you in these verses?

JOSEPH FINALLY SEES BENJAMIN

Imagine the myriad of emotions that stirred within Joseph as he sees his brother Benjamin for the first time in twenty years. The last time Joseph saw him, Benjamin had been a boy (scholars generally agree that Benjamin was somewhere between six and ten years younger than Joseph). Benjamin is now a grown man. What had his life been like?

When my grandmother passed away when I was about eighteen years old, our family made the twelve-hour drive to Arkansas from Texas together to attend the funeral. Grandmother had been ill with Alzheimer's for many years, so my sisters and I had not seen her for a very long time. My dad did not want us to experience the moment when my grandmother did not recognize us any longer like he had. (My dad carried those painful memories of not being recognized by his mother for years.)

While we were there, dad's entire family gathered, and, similar to most funerals, it turned into sort of a family reunion. I was reunited with cousins I had not seen in ten years—Beth, in particular. She was the closest to me in age and we had played together often as kids when my family had visited during Christmastime and long summer holidays.

I remember that I kept staring at Beth, trying to recognize voice inflections, facial features, and personality characteristics of the girl I used to play with as a child. Eventually, it all came rushing back and we spent much time together that weekend. I did not realize how much I had missed her until I saw her again.

Have you ever been parted from a loved one for an extended period of time? If so, how did you feel when you were reunited?

What questions did you want to ask them?

Joseph likely had so many questions for Benjamin. But he restrains himself and decides to invite his brothers to his home for lunch, away from the transaction-centered, businesslike atmosphere of the palace. After all, what better way to observe his brothers than to enjoy a relaxing meal together?

THE BROTHERS PLEAD INNOCENT

Read Genesis 43:18–25. What is the first reaction of Joseph's brothers to the change of venue?

Why were they afraid?

In ancient civilizations, an invitation to dine with the ruler was the highest honor extended to visiting dignitaries or honored guests. In fact, that still holds true today. This would be tantamount to receiving an invitation from the White House to enjoy dinner in the president's private residence.

Yet such an unexpected change of venue terrifies the brothers. They are strangers from a foreign land who have already been treated roughly by Joseph. They cannot conceive how this sudden change could bode well for their grain mission.

Their guilt rises to the surface, and they scramble to explain to the steward what had happened regarding the money found in their sacks. They make it absolutely clear that they had no intention of stealing grain. To bolster their argument, they confirm that they have brought the original money plus additional money for the second round of grain. You can almost feel the panic in their chests.

In Genesis 43:23, how does the steward reply?

Do not be afraid. We are reminded of those calm-inducing words over and over again throughout Scripture. Usually, they are spoken by an angel or the Lord Himself. The archangel Gabriel told Mary not to be afraid when she learned she would be the mother of our Savior (see Luke 1:30). In the Upper Room, Jesus told His disciples not to let their hearts be troubled or afraid (see John 14:27). And He still speaks that assurance over us today.

Write out Psalm 56:3.

This is an excellent verse to memorize and plaster over every surface near you. When we struggle in times of uncertainty and fear the worst, this verse (and many others like it) reminds us that God's got us. He never abandons us to the panic that fear can induce.

For Joseph's brothers, the steward is the one who speaks the Lord's peace over them to ease their fears. And as if to prove the truth of his words, the steward has Simeon brought out. What a relief to see their brother unharmed, alive, and well!

Have you ever needed tangible proof to ease a particular fear? If so, what was the situation?

What was the tangible proof that God provided?

In June 2020, my sister Monica was in a car accident and sustained life-threatening injuries after hitting the windshield. She was rushed by ambulance to the hospital while the police called my older sister, Elisabeth, to let her know what had happened. When Elisabeth called to relay the news to me, I literally jumped out of my chair while she was still talking to grab my keys and race to the hospital.

However, the pandemic had just reared its ugly head and the hospital was shut down to visitors. Panic filled my chest as I tried to figure out a way to get to Monica's side. I could not heal her, but I could certainly hold her hand, pray over her, and tell her how much we loved her. Thinking of her alone was absolutely gut-wrenching.

Thankfully, Elisabeth is an emergency room nurse. Although she did not work at the hospital where Monica had been taken, she pulled professional strings to gain access. I cannot tell you the wave of relief and tears that flooded out of my soul when Elisabeth called from Monica's bedside. Monica would live, but she was paralyzed from the neck down.

Since Monica's condition was so severe, the hospital relaxed the rules to allow one visitor per day. After three days, I was finally able to see her. I broke down and ugly cried. Finally, I had tangible proof that she would survive because I was able to hold her hand and tell her how much I loved her. Fast forward past months of physical therapy to today. Monica has regained 90 percent of her mobility and leads a very normal life. Thank You, Lord!

Sometimes we just need tangible proof when fear threatens to engulf us. Like holding a loved one's hand. Like hearing a dear friend's voice. Like seeing an empty tomb on Easter morning.

DINING WITH THE PRIME MINISTER

Read Genesis 43:26–34.

After receiving water, having their feet washed, and knowing that their animals had been cared for, the brothers let go of fear and settled down to enjoy the meal. As soon as Joseph enters, we see his old dream play out again in real time as his brothers—all eleven of them this time—bow down before him.

In Genesis 43:27, what is the first question that Joseph asks?

Unbeknownst to the brothers, they have passed the first portion of Joseph's test. Benjamin is all right. But now the test continues as Joseph asks about his father. After receiving assurance that his father is also well, Joseph finally turns his eyes to his younger brother. Benjamin has Joseph's full attention.

And after blessing Benjamin, Joseph is overcome with emotion for a second time and has to excuse himself to regain composure. The first time it happened, he overheard his older brothers acknowledge responsibility for what they had done to him twenty years ago. Now this second time, Joseph is overcome by seeing that his only full brother is truly safe and by hearing that his father is alive and well.

Finally, after twenty years apart, Joseph sits down to have a meal in the same room as his brothers. And then something astonishing happens.

In Genesis 43:33, how were the brothers seated?

How could this Egyptian prime minister know the order of their births and seat them accordingly? And they were amazed. As the brothers sit at their table, Joseph sits at his, and the Egyptians sit at theirs, everyone settles down to enjoy the meal.

In Genesis 43:34, how much larger is Benjamin's portion than his brothers?

This is yet another way that Joseph tests his brothers. Since favoritism and jealousy caused his older brothers to sell him into slavery twenty years ago, Joseph tests them here to see if overgenerosity to Benjamin brings out those old behaviors. Thankfully, the older brothers pass this test as well, and they are able to eat, drink, and be merry together.

At one time or another in our lives, each of us has secretly tested family, friends, or acquaintances to determine if their walk matches their talk.

Thankfully, we never have to wonder about our Lord and Savior, Jesus Christ. He walked all the way to Calvary on our behalf and took the punishment we deserved. No hesitation. No excuses.

He alone "is the same yesterday and today and forever" (Hebrews 13:8).

Go Quiet, Go Deep

Quiet your mind from distractions and pull your Bible close. Bow your head and ask Jesus to make His Word and today's lesson personal for you.

Take your time writing out Isaiah 25:6.

What does it mean to you personally that regardless of what you have done on earth, one day you will dine at the Lord's banquet table?

I pray that the boundless love, grace, and forgiveness of Jesus would penetrate every barrier today so that He can work in you and through you.

WEEK 5

TESTS OF FAITH

Genesis 44–45

Finally, we see the forgiving grace of God. As nine scared brothers plus Benjamin return to Egypt seeking food, a forgiving God was seeking them. Joseph administers a few more tests on his brothers, which they pass. When all is said and done, and with cinematic flair befitting an Oscar performance, Joseph finally reveals his identity as their long-lost brother.

Gratitude replaces terror as the brothers realize that Joseph intends to restore their relationship. Everything Joseph put his brothers through since they came to Egypt was intended to bring them to a place where they could believe and receive his forgiveness. For you and me, believing and receiving God's forgiveness is crucial toward healing. Grace, forgiveness, fruits of blessing, and celebration of life flow beautifully from this chapter.

DAY 1   The Test *(Genesis 44:1–13)*

DAY 2   Standing in the Gap *(Genesis 44:14–34)*

DAY 3   Forgiveness and Grace *(Genesis 45:1–15)*

DAY 4   The Fruits of Blessing *(Genesis 45:16–23)*

DAY 5   The Celebration of Life *(Genesis 45:24–28)*

KEY QUESTIONS:

- What steps do you take when you struggle with self-pity?

- If you have had to forgive a deep hurt, how did God direct your journey?

- When it comes to reconciliation, how intentional are you?

DAY 1

THE TEST

As soon as the morning was light, the men were sent away with their donkeys. They had gone only a short distance from the city. Now Joseph said to his steward, "Up, follow after the men, and when you overtake them, say to them, 'Why have you repaid evil for good? Is it not from this that my lord drinks, and by this that he practices divination? You have done evil in doing this.'" (Genesis 44:3–5)

Tests of faith are uncomfortable. Most often, we would rather not participate. But they are sent by our loving God as a tool for our spiritual growth. Thankfully, God never tempts us toward failure. That's what the devil does. God tests us to reveal areas in our lives where we need to repent and trust Him to make us more like Christ. That is a huge difference.

Read Genesis 44:1–10. What stands out to you in these verses?

FALSELY ACCUSED

At first glance, this may seem like Joseph is taking revenge on his older brothers for selling him into slavery when he was seventeen. His action seems like a devious trick to set up his brothers and ensnare them without escape. However, Joseph not only returned all of the brothers' money from both trips to their sacks but he also instructs that his own silver cup be placed in Benjamin's sack. We can almost hear the dramatic tympani roll building in the background!

In Genesis 44:7, what is the last statement that the brothers say to Joseph's steward?

Far be it from us! No one likes to be falsely accused, and the brothers are no different. Even though they had certainly been deceitful in the past, in this instance, they are completely innocent.

Have you ever been falsely accused of wrongdoing? If so, how did that make you feel?

What happened?

What did God show you through that experience?

I tend to drive like I'm running from the devil. It's also true that living in Houston makes for tough-skinned drivers. Let's just say that if I am on a schedule, I simply like to get where I'm going expediently. On those occasions that I get pulled over, nine times out of ten, I am flat-out guilty. However, the one time out of ten that I am innocent, my nose gets out of joint.

In those moments, I proclaim my innocence loud and clear to set the record straight. But the truth is that I deserve a ticket just about every time I get behind the wheel of my vehicle. Whether it's speeding, not coming to a full stop before turning right, or something else, I have received grace countless times by not being caught.

The reality is that I (and all of us) are guilty of far greater offense than speeding or telling little white lies. We make ourselves comfortable by thinking that sin is far from us. *Far be it from me!* But the truth is that sin resides within us. Even if we are innocent in certain moments, we are guilty in totality because of the sin that flows freely out of our hearts every day. It took the blood of Jesus to cleanse us for all time.

Jesus knows what it feels like to be wrongly accused. Throughout the Gospels, Jesus was routinely accused of all manner of wrongdoing (of which He was completely innocent), including blasphemy, sedition, sorcery, self-aggrandizing behavior, leading people astray, and many other false accusations.

How is Jesus described in the following verses?

1 Peter 2:22

Hebrews 4:15

Jesus did not bother responding to false accusations because His mission was so much bigger than proving His own innocence in the moment. Jesus was also judged harshly regarding His actions in other situations, which offers us abundant hope regarding our relationship with Him. What do the following verses tell us?

In John 8:10–11, what did Jesus say to the woman caught in adultery?

In Mark 2:17, how did Jesus respond when the Pharisees questioned why Jesus ate with sinners and tax collectors?

The woman, sinners, and tax collectors had been rightly accused. We are also guilty as charged of having sinned and fallen short of the glory of God (see Romans 3:23). But, by the grace of God, that is not the end of our story in Christ.

A VOW OF BRAVADO

Although Joseph's brothers become indignant at being falsely accused, the truth is that they have done far worse deeds in the past than stealing a silver cup. Their response reveals the dark heart of a sinner. *Far be it from me!* In reality, they had not just allegedly stolen a silver cup from Joseph; *they had actually stolen his entire life.* Yet they still had the nerve to act offended when accused of a far less serious crime.

As the brothers attempt to defend themselves against the steward's charge, they make a very foolish statement.

In Genesis 44:9, what do the brothers vow?

Wouldn't you love to know the steward's thoughts at that point? The steward already knew they would be found guilty because he was the person who planted the silver cup in their possession! So now comes the unveiling.

THE SILVER CUP TEST

Read Genesis 44:11–13.

Believing they will be fully cleared of the steward's false accusations, their mouths hit the ground in astonishment as the silver cup is indeed found among them. Frankly, they should have known better than randomly agreeing to open their sacks for inspection. Remember the money bags they discovered in their sacks after their first journey to Egypt? But in their haste to prove their innocence, they forget that very important detail. Or perhaps the suspense was too much.

In whose sack is Joseph's silver cup discovered?

You can't help but feel a bit sorry for the brothers at this point. I imagine their mouths opening and closing several times, their minds scrambling to find a plausible explanation. But they were at a loss for words. Here they stand caught between a rock and a hard place.

Although the brothers believed they were in serious trouble with Egypt's prime minister, that was likely not their greatest fear at that point. Their father's worst-case scenario had become a reality: *Benjamin, Jacob's favorite son, was in danger.*

Ironically enough, that is Joseph's intent during this particular test. Under the threat of losing Benjamin forever, the brothers would be forced to recall what Joseph had endured at their hands more than twenty years previously. Joseph's goal is not their destruction but to bring them to a place of repentance in hopes of restoring their relationship.

So the brothers loaded their donkeys and turned their mounts back to Egypt.

JUDGMENT DAY

In an attempt to avoid judgment, the older brothers had used careless and rash words that actually condemned them. The silver cup was found, they were deemed guilty, and all returned to Egypt to face judgment.

As we close, there is an important parallel here that we need to grasp. On Judgment Day, every human being will stand before Christ. What will happen according to the following verses?

Matthew 12:37

Revelation 20:11–15

While in this life, you and I have the opportunity to repent of our sins and receive God's forgiveness. When we stand before Christ's throne in heaven, we will be rendered silent as every thought, word, and deed throughout our entire lives will be brought to light.

What does Romans 3:19–20 reveal?

Even as I recall the thoughts that ran through my mind just today, it will be horrifying to hear them read aloud on Judgment Day. What about you? It will be too late to offer any defense or rebut the evidence when we stand before the throne of Jesus in heaven. The Law will find us guilty as charged and deserving of hell.

But not on His watch.

Those who are in Christ will not be condemned under the Law.

Jesus was silent as a sheep before the shearers in front of His accusers on the day of His earthly judgment. Yet He carried every single one of our sins upon Himself to that wooden cross on Good Friday. Our sins were the nails that pierced His hands and feet and the spear that pierced His side.

And as Jesus died, rose again from the dead, and took His place at the right hand of God in heaven, He now stands *as eternal surety for us.*

Regardless of how careless our words, rash our actions, or lengthy our list of wrongdoings on Judgment Day, Christ will pronounce only one verdict over every life that His blood redeemed:

Forgiven. "He will wipe away every tear from their eyes, and death shall be no more, neither shall there be mourning, nor crying, nor pain anymore, for the former things have passed away. And He who was seated on the throne said, 'Behold, I am making all things new'" (Revelation 21:4–5a).

Amazing grace. How sweet the sound!

Go Quiet, Go Deep

Quiet your mind from distractions and pull your Bible close. Bow your head and ask Jesus to make His Word and today's lesson personal for you.

Take your time writing out Psalm 107:2–3.

What does it mean to you personally that as a redeemed child of God, He wants you to tell your story?

I pray that the boundless love, grace, and forgiveness of Jesus would penetrate every barrier today so that He can work in you and through you.

DAY 2

STANDING IN THE GAP

Now therefore, please let your servant remain instead of the boy as a servant to my lord, and let the boy go back with his brothers. (Genesis 44:33)

In our lesson on Day 1, we left off with the brothers returning to Egypt and being found guilty of theft after the steward discovered Joseph's silver cup. However, as is customary with many Old Testament narratives, one sentence often contains considerable unspoken drama. And we find that here, as well.

Write out Genesis 44:13.

Now try to imagine the emotion and drama of that moment. As the steward methodically opens each sack, perhaps the brothers feel confidence in their innocence rising after each search turns up empty. Maybe they begin to breathe a little easier. They might just make it! Then, as the steward opens the last sack, the morning sun catches the glint of a silver cup peeking out of Benjamin's sack. *Oh no, not Benjamin!*

So, the brothers tore their clothes. This phrase appears throughout the Old Testament as a sign of great grief, mourning, or extreme distress. To grasp how distressing this moment was for the brothers, let's look at a few examples.

In Job 1:13–20, what happens to cause Job to tear his robe in great grief?

In 2 Samuel 13:30–31, why does King David tear his clothes in extreme distress?

At that moment, when Joseph's brothers tore their clothes before heading back to Egypt, they were experiencing great distress. Even though being found guilty of theft and its looming consequences were distressing, their greatest distress regarded Benjamin's fate.

STANDING BEFORE JOSEPH ONCE AGAIN

Read Genesis 44:14–15. What does Joseph ask his brothers in Genesis 44:15?

Now, let's be clear. Joseph is not admitting to being a magician or sorcerer. Joseph is making the point that the brothers should realize a man in his position has abundant resources to find out anything he wants to know. In our modern context, it would be like the head of the FBI. Spies with eyes, a notepad, and a cell phone ready to learn and expose every detail.

Egypt's rulers, like other pagan nations, relied on the use of diviners and magicians. In fact, the failure of those very people around Pharaoh is how Joseph became prime minister (see Genesis 41:8).

However, there is no indication anywhere in Joseph's narrative that he routinely practiced any kind of divination or sorcery. Joseph simply leveraged those particular vocations in order to add yet another layer of distress to his brothers to bring them to repentance. Then Judah steps up to the mic.

JUDAH SPEAKS UP

Read Genesis 44:16–17. What is the first question that Judah asks in Genesis 44:16?

What shall we say? In other words, they had been caught red-handed. No forensic tests were needed because the cup was found in Benjamin's sack in front of everybody. How many times have you asked that same question if you've been caught red-handed?

At one point in our childhood, my sisters refused to play Monopoly® with me. I would always insist on being the banker and then routinely slip extra $500 bills into my stack of money so I could buy the most property. When my sisters inevitably caught me red-handed, I would ask, "What can I say?" and laugh, then put the ill-gotten gains back in the bank. Thankfully, God has since taught me the value of honest competition.

Judah asks, "What shall we say?" But he is not laughing. Judah understood the high stakes in play at that moment. It was literally life versus death. Freedom versus slavery. His father's well-being versus his despair.

What else does Judah say to Joseph in Genesis 44:16?

Joseph must be wondering what point Judah is working toward with this speech. When Joseph was ready to take Benjamin as a prisoner and let the brothers come and go freely, it was the exact place they had been twenty-some years before. Would they value their own freedom and forsake Benjamin as they had forsaken Joseph?

Joseph's test for his brothers is pretty straightforward—will the brothers confirm Benjamin's guilt so they are released, or will they barter for Benjamin's life? To find out which, Joseph drives his point home a little deeper.

How does he respond to Judah in Genesis 44:17?

Joseph keeps the test going as he brings the full weight of their situation down onto their shoulders. But Judah may be thinking, *Peace to my father?* From what we have learned about Jacob and his intense love for Benjamin, there will not be one bit of peace if the brothers return home without Benjamin. They would rather remain slaves in Egypt!

Perhaps here, Judah finally recognizes the hand of God in this whole situation. Even though he and his brothers are innocent of stealing Joseph's silver cup, they are guilty of stealing the life Joseph could have had in Canaan over twenty years ago.

JUDAH'S PLEA

Read Genesis 44:18–34.

Judah takes time to carefully retell the events that happened from the time Jacob sent the brothers to Egypt the first time to buy grain up to the present moment.

We need to remember that Judah still has no clue that he is addressing his long-lost brother, Joseph. In his mind, the person he addresses is a high Egyptian official possessing Pharaoh's authority and power to either destroy them or save them.

So Judah attempts to get this official to understand the depth and breadth of their suffering. What Judah fails to realize is that there is *no one else* who can understand that particular suffering better than Joseph.

Judah includes all of the emotion and distress that has accompanied their journey but repeatedly refers to their father's suffering. *Four times*, Judah mentions how his father would suffer if they were to return from Egypt without Benjamin.

Which four verses in Genesis 44:16–34 refer to Jacob's suffering?

Judah attempts to make it clear that if Joseph punishes Benjamin, he would be punishing the innocent along with the guilty, for Benjamin's father would surely die. So Judah offers something extraordinary.

SUBSTITUTIONARY SACRIFICE

What does Judah offer to Joseph in verse 33?

Judah is not asking Joseph to overlook guilt, leave it unpunished, or look the other way. Instead, Judah offers *himself*. He does not ask Joseph to let it slide; he asks Joseph to make him a substitute. Without verbalizing it directly, Judah tells Joseph, "Punish me, instead."

Judah offers his life as surety to secure Benjamin's freedom. The significance of this moment cannot be overstated. As one of Jacob's twelve sons, Judah formed one of the twelve tribes of Israel: the tribe of Judah. Judah's tribe was symbolized by a lion, according to Jacob's prophetic blessing before Jacob died (see Genesis 49:9).

The listing of Jesus' genealogy in Matthew 1 begins, "Abraham was the father of Isaac, and Isaac the father of Jacob, and Jacob the father of Judah and his brothers" (Matthew 1:2). Here, the Gospel writer shows that Jesus is descended from the tribe of Judah.

Write out Revelation 5:5.

Jesus is our Lion of Judah! He is descended through the line of Judah. As Judah had offered his life to Joseph as a substitute to save Benjamin from punishment, Jesus offered His life to our heavenly Father as a substitutionary sacrifice to save you and me from eternal punishment.

The Lion of Judah is our conquering, victorious King. He voluntarily took our place on the criminal's cross! He fulfilled every prophecy and promise contained in Scripture. He is the Alpha and Omega, the beginning and the end. He is the only answer we need to every single challenge we will ever face.

Even when it seems like we only have bad options to choose from in a difficult situation, we can have full confidence and trust in Jesus. He is our deliverer, who came to set the captives free. He alone conquered our death, our sin, and our grave.

His love and blessings for His children far exceed anything that we can hope for or imagine because He cares for us.

As Judah kept his promise to his father, Jacob, to stand surety for Benjamin, so Jesus kept His promise to our Father in heaven to stand surety for us.

Our Lion of Judah is trustworthy and is mighty to save!

Go Quiet, Go Deep

Quiet your mind from distractions and pull your Bible close. Bow your head and ask Jesus to make His Word and today's lesson personal for you.

Take your time writing out 1 Thessalonians 5:9–10.

What does it mean to you personally that Jesus took your place on the cross so that you can be with Him in eternity?

I pray that the boundless love, grace, and forgiveness of Jesus would penetrate every barrier today so that He can work in you and through you.

DAY 3

FORGIVENESS AND GRACE

So Joseph said to his brothers, "Come near to me, please." And they came near. And he said, "I am your brother, Joseph, whom you sold into Egypt. And now do not be distressed or angry with yourselves because you sold me here, for God sent me before you to preserve life." (Genesis 45:4–5)

Years ago, when my youngest sister wanted to get out into the world after graduating from high school, she asked if she could share an apartment with me. Since my current apartment lease was nearly up, I agreed. It would be so fun to have her as a roommate!

However, her job's salary was insufficient to secure the rental lease, so I stood surety for her. Standing as surety means you offer yourself (or your resources) as security for the fulfillment of someone else's obligation or debt.

In other words, whether or not my sister could pay her portion of the rent, I was responsible to the apartment company for the entire amount. Standing surety released her from financial responsibility and placed the burden on me. However, it was a no-brainer, and I gladly signed on the dotted line. We truly had a blast rooming together and bonded even closer. It was a huge blessing in our lives.

Have you ever been asked to stand surety for anyone? If so, what was it?

How did the situation turn out?

We ended our last lesson with Judah's dramatic and extraordinary offer to stand surety for Benjamin. In offering to take Benjamin's place to secure his freedom, Judah was willing to take on his brother's punishment.

Usually, loved ones or only those closest to us will ask us to stand surety for them. We often gladly offer to help because we know, love, and trust them. But would you stand surety for your enemies?

That is exactly what Jesus did. Regardless of how recklessly we live, how carelessly we handle our resources, or whether we faithfully keep all of the Ten Commandments, Jesus offered His life as surety. His surety released us from facing God's wrath on Judgement Day and placed the burden squarely on His shoulders on Good Friday. There is no greater surety.

JOSEPH BREAKS DOWN
Read Genesis 45:1–3. What stands out to you in these verses?

Up to this point, Joseph has kept his identity concealed. He has spoken through interpreters to avoid vocal recognition. Except for the meal shared at the end of Genesis 43, Joseph has generally dealt roughly with his brothers.

Unbeknownst to them, Joseph has been methodically testing his brothers to bring them to a fresh awareness of their sin. Joseph's actions were not simply to berate them for what they did, but to bring about repentance to repair their broken family relationship. Joseph needed to determine if they were still the same self-centered, jealous brothers who sold him into slavery two decades before.

In Genesis 45:1, what does Joseph command?

Imagine that moment! Here is the second most powerful man in all of Egypt suddenly becoming so emotional that he demands everyone clear the room except for himself and the eleven other Hebrew men.

We can picture the servants scrambling in their haste to leave and waiting attentively just outside the door. And while they wait, they hear their leader wailing at the top of his lungs. Just imagine! Was he in trouble? Was he safe? What in the *world* was happening?

Martin Luther observed:

> [Joseph] cannot contain himself any longer after he sees that their heart is sincere, that their prayer is steadfast, and that the love of Judah and his brothers for Benjamin is not feigned but is joined with true penitence. For this is an example not only of prayer but of true and very great penitence.[12]

With only Joseph and his brothers in the room, Joseph makes his astonishing revelation.

What does Joseph finally reveal in Genesis 45:3?

Joseph's announcement has to be without a doubt the most startling words his brothers have ever heard in their entire lives.

How do the brothers react at the end of Genesis 45:3?

Just imagine how many thoughts and questions likely bombarded their minds all at once!

Joseph? Our brother, Joseph?

Did he just speak Hebrew?

He could understand what we were saying the whole time?

I thought his name was Zaphenath-paneah?

I wonder if he still holds a grudge against us.

We're toast.

These brothers have already experienced an emotional roller coaster. The silver cup was found in Benjamin's sack. They returned to Egypt as thieves. Benjamin is in danger, and Judah just offered to switch places with him. It appears that the brothers are about to lose another brother. How could things possibly get more dramatic?

They never expected that this powerful Egyptian official would say in their native Hebrew language: "I am *Joseph*." It's a wonder that they all just didn't pass out at that point. What a shock! The brothers expect the worst punishment and are numbed into silence. Fear often does that to us.

When is the last time fear caused you to be silent?

What happened?

Joseph's brothers have difficulty reconciling what their eyes see against what their ears hear. The person they see before them is dressed in Egypt's finest clothes, groomed like an Egyptian, and exudes all the power and authority of an Egyptian prime minister. Yet their ears hear a voice they haven't heard in more than twenty years—that of their brother Joseph.

After revealing his identity, what is the first question Joseph asks?

Like any child who is deeply loved by his parents and loves them in return, Joseph just wants to know if his dad is okay.

Have you ever been put in the position of asking someone if your mom or dad is okay?

When my dad struggled with cancer, I constantly wondered if he was doing okay. Since he was often too sick or weak to talk at length, I checked in with my mom on a regular basis. Were the treatments working? Was he terribly sick? Would he be all right? I could do nothing to change dad's situation, but at least knowing the answers informed my prayers.

JOSEPH RECONCILES WITH HIS BROTHERS
Read Genesis 45:4–13.

Joseph's revelation has startled his brothers into silence. So Joseph *asks*—not commands—that his brothers come near. Joseph realizes that if he wants an answer to his burning question, he needs a less dramatic approach. Perhaps his voice and demeanor were gentler. And he asks them to draw near.

In Genesis 45:4–11, what are some of the key items that Joseph tells his brothers?

The overarching and most startling thing Joseph reveals is that he does not hold his brothers accountable for selling him into slavery. Joseph extends to his older brothers the grace that he never received from them.

This is one of the most beautiful examples in all of Scripture of what forgiveness sounds like and looks like.

I am Joseph, your brother, whom you sold into Egypt, *but I do not seek revenge.*

God sent me to Egypt to preserve your life, *not to destroy it.*

You sold my life for twenty pieces of silver, *but your freedom will cost you nothing.*

For you and me, hearing forgiveness from Jesus might sound like this:

I am Jesus, your Savior, whom you often push aside, *but I do not seek revenge.*

God sent me to earth to preserve your life, *not to destroy it.*

My life was sold for thirty pieces of silver, *but your freedom will cost you nothing.*

What does Jesus tell His disciples in Mark 11:25?

Forgiveness and grace are two of the most power-packed, life-giving words spoken over our lives by our Savior. He extends both to us in endless supply. And Joseph's brothers received both that day as well.

In Genesis 45:9–11, what does Joseph ask his brothers to tell their father, Jacob?

Finally, overcome with emotion, Joseph clings to his brother Benjamin and weeps. Then he kisses each brother and weeps some more.

And unlike that of Judas Iscariot, Joseph's kiss was one of joyful restoration.

Go Quiet, Go Deep

Quiet your mind from distractions and pull your Bible close. Bow your head and ask Jesus to make His Word and today's lesson personal for you.

Take your time writing out Ephesians 2:8.

What does it mean to you personally that by the grace of God you are completely forgiven?

I pray that the boundless love, grace, and forgiveness of Jesus would penetrate every barrier today so that He can work in you and through you.

DAY 4

THE FRUITS OF BLESSING

When the report was heard in Pharaoh's house, "Joseph's brothers have come," it pleased Pharaoh and his servants. And Pharaoh said to Joseph, "Say to your brothers, 'Do this: load your beasts and go back to the land of Canaan, and take your father and your households, and come to me, and I will give you the best of the land of Egypt, and you shall eat the fat of the land.'" (Genesis 45:16–18)

During the years that I worked at the law firm, each time I was assigned to work with a new partner or associate, I would immediately jump on the internet. I searched their work history, law school activities, bar association involvement, and social media connections. I wanted to know as much as I could about their work ethic, stability, achievements, and community advocacy to get a sense of their character and background.

However, the most important thing without fail was actually getting to know them once they joined the firm. Learning firsthand what inspired and challenged them, their work habits, and their personality type was vital to determine how we could work best as a team.

We can only assume that Pharaoh performed some kind of reconnaissance on Joseph once he had been appointed prime minister. It is hard to fathom that a wise leader in such a vital role would neglect to learn the background and history of his right-hand man. And Pharaoh's staff and servants likely questioned among themselves why Joseph had been promoted and elevated above all others for such an honored position.

Although Scripture is silent, it is plausible that Pharaoh and his staff knew more than the fact that Joseph simply came from prison. For starters, he was Hebrew and not Egyptian. That alone would raise curiosity. So those surrounding Joseph probably had some knowledge of his estrangement from his brothers—especially if they inquired how he came to be in Egypt and prison in the first place.

When Joseph finally revealed his identity to his brothers, he wept over them and wailed so loudly that "the Egyptians heard it, and the household of

Pharaoh heard it" (Genesis 45:2). They must have been thoroughly alarmed until they discovered the reason.

A NEW DAY

Read Genesis 45:16–20. How did Pharaoh and his servants react to Joseph's news in Genesis 45:16?

That they were pleased for Joseph indicates that Joseph was probably well liked or highly respected. We are usually not pleased when something good happens to snarky people, right? We tend to celebrate when good things happen to good people. That's just human nature.

In Genesis 45:18, what does Pharaoh offer?

Pharaoh's generosity reveals how much he favored Joseph. Let's face it, without Joseph's accurate interpretation of Pharaoh's dreams and diligent work to preserve Egypt's resources in preparation for the current famine, Pharaoh would be ruler over scorpions and a whole lot of sand.

Can you imagine the extent of Joseph's joy upon hearing Pharaoh's generous offer? He had been alone in Egypt without his family of origin for over two decades. Now, thanks to Pharaoh's compassionate generosity, Joseph's entire family would be a short chariot ride away in Goshen for the rest of his life.

Family is God's idea. He never intended for us to walk alone through life with all of its ups and downs. How do you see that truth in the following verses?

Genesis 2:18

Genesis 4:1–2

Psalm 127:3

A loving, close-knit family is one of God's great blessings to us. Granted, not everyone enjoys such a relationship with their family—including Joseph for many years. He had a wife and two sons, but they are not the same as the people who had known him since birth. Those few who know our whole history and know us the best hold a special place in our hearts and memories.

In my early years, I did not have a best friend until I reached high school. Even though people hinted that it was unusual to *not* have one, I never felt like I was missing out. Looking back, I realize now that my three sisters were my best friends. I had no need to look beyond the walls of my home to find the people I most wanted to spend my time and life with.

To a very large extent, that remains true today. My sisters and I love escaping our daily responsibilities for special sister days (like going to a home show, gardening show, concert, or other fun pursuits) or going on sisters-only trips. In December 2016, we secured a regular cabin for a four-day cruise to the Bahamas. The four of us were absolutely crammed in that cabin together, but we loved the uninterrupted time to catch up and enjoy an adventure together.

THE FRUITS OF BLESSING
Read Genesis 45:21–23.

Recall verse 16. Again, it is likely that Joseph was a respected and well-liked member of Pharoah's kingdom. However, the greater point of these passages is that we all delight when genuine reconciliation takes place. What do the following verses say about reconciliation?

Romans 5:10–11

Colossians 1:21–22

Reconciliation eliminates separation, melts hostility, and brings peace. It is the very heart of the Gospel. In our sin, we were hostile to God and were His enemies. And even though we chose not to move toward God, He chose to move toward us with the greatest love ever known.

You and I did not lift a finger toward reconciliation and certainly did not deserve it. We did nothing to deserve such lavish generosity from God except receive it by the faith that He alone provides. Reconciliation was so important to God that He leveraged His Son in our place.

Joseph had been estranged from his brothers for so many years. And now, they are embracing and weeping with joy at being reunited.

Have you ever witnessed or experienced such a reconciliation? How did it impact your faith?

When hate is conquered by love, we rejoice! It is such a beautiful picture of what Jesus accomplished for us.

What does 2 Corinthians 5:18–21 tell us?

Because of His great love for us and by shedding His blood in our place, Jesus reconciled us back to God. Rejoice!

THE BEST IS YET TO COME

Joseph relates Pharaoh's words to his brothers (who are probably stunned again) and the relocation preparation begins. Did you notice that Pharaoh went the extra mile? He did not just instruct Joseph to relocate them and make him manage the process.

In Genesis 45:19–20, Pharaoh also provides transportation for their families. Carts and wagons for their possessions. And he reassures Joseph that if they have to leave anything behind, the abundance of Egypt will provide replacements. As for us, we can take none of our possessions with us when we die, but we don't need to—the abundance of our Father's house will be sufficient for us.

What an incredible turn of events in such a short time frame.

The brothers return to Egypt expecting punishment and wrath.

They leave reconciled with Joseph with the best of Egypt awaiting their arrival.

On Easter morning, you and I experienced an incredible turn of events.

We deserved God's punishment and wrath.

We are reconciled to God with the best of eternity awaiting our arrival because of Christ's sacrifice and great love for us.

Grace upon grace.

Go Quiet, Go Deep

Quiet your mind from distractions and pull your Bible close. Bow your head and ask Jesus to make His Word and today's lesson personal for you.

Take your time writing out 2 Corinthians 5:18–19.

What does it mean to you personally that Jesus has reconciled you to God?

I pray that the boundless love, grace, and forgiveness of Jesus would penetrate every barrier today so that He can work in you and through you.

DAY 5

THE CELEBRATION OF LIFE

So they went up out of Egypt and came to the land of Canaan to their father Jacob. (Genesis 45:25)

W ith a few parting words from Joseph, the brothers set out to rescue Jacob and their families from famine, loaded with gifts and abundant provisions for the journey to Egypt. Little did Jacob know that when he woke up that morning, he would discover that his long-lost, favorite son, Joseph, was still alive. And not only alive but one of the most powerful men in Egypt.

GETTING ALONG

Read Genesis 45:24–28. What stands out to you in those verses?

What is Joseph's parting statement to his brothers in Genesis 45:24?

Why do you believe Joseph said that?

The verb *quarrel* here (זָגַר) means to be agitated or perturbed. We have only to look back to Genesis 37 to see how agitated and perturbed Joseph's brothers can be. Joseph wants his parting words to reverberate in his brothers' minds as they leave Egypt. They have just shared a beautiful reconciliation and newfound peace. Joseph is telling them, "Now don't mess it up!"

Besides children, have you ever needed to tell someone not to be quarrelsome? If so, what happened?

Has someone ever said those words to you?

As a person who tends to be a tad impatient and impulsive, I am often the recipient of various forms of that phrase. Most of the time, I do not realize I am being impatient or curt until someone I love says, "Hey, whoa, it's going to be okay" or "Calm down."

Although it does not feel good to hear such admonitions (my first instinct is usually to defend myself), their words cause me to pause. I start to listen more closely to what I'm saying and the tone I'm using. What do the following verses say about our words?

Ephesians 4:29

Proverbs 12:18

Words matter. And Joseph picks them wisely. *Don't quarrel.* Perhaps he was attempting to cause his brothers to pause and listen to their words before speaking. The text does not say how the brothers reacted to Joseph's parting words. No roll of the eyes or rebuttal is recorded, and they arrive back in Canaan without issue.

THE BROTHERS' UNSPOKEN DILEMMA

Here again, we come across an Old Testament event that is encapsulated in just a few sentences, yet much drama happens offstage (figuratively speaking). As the brothers journey home, they face an unspoken dilemma. On one hand, they get to tell their father that Joseph is alive and prospering. On the other hand, they have to explain to their father *why* Joseph is alive.

In Genesis 45:26, what is Jacob's reaction to hearing the news?

In Hebrew, the word used to describe what Jacob experienced as his heart became numb (פּוּג) indicates that he felt cold, void of warmth, and not moved with joy. In other words, he could not properly function after hearing such startling words. He does not believe them. It is simply too much to take in. He is *numb*.

I have prayed with and walked beside friends who have lost children through miscarriage, accidents, or suicide. It takes a *very* long time (often a lifetime) of walking through an intensely painful grieving process to come to terms with the earthly loss of a child. If this is such a season for you, my heartfelt sorrow and prayers go out to you during this process of healing.

In Genesis 45:27, what do the brothers tell their father?

Did you notice that they omit any reference whatsoever to *how* Joseph is alive? They simply tell Jacob what Joseph asked them to relay and then point out the wagons and goods that Joseph sent along. The rest of Joseph's narrative reveals that the brothers never confessed to their father the part they played in Joseph's disappearance twenty years before.

Confession is an integral part of our faith journey. When we confess our sins to God, He removes our guilt and sin and restores our intimate fellowship with Him. What do the following verses tell us about confession?

Proverbs 28:13

Acts 3:19

James 5:16

Over the years, I have come to realize that confession includes two specific elements: (1) the confession of my sins, and (2) the receiving of God's forgiveness—that is, admitting my dependence on God. When we wholeheartedly confess our sins to God, we can depend on Him to restore the fellowship with Him that our sin broke.

Scripture tells us that we are to continually confess our sins, understanding that because of Jesus' work on our behalf, God has *already* extended forgiveness. God faithfully and unconditionally extends forgiveness, whether a person confesses and believes or not. However, when we do not acknowledge a sin we are aware of committing, we experience shame and end up hiding from God. Remember Adam and Eve in the Garden of Eden? If we want to experience that relief and release from that sin, then we must confess it to God and repent of it and then receive God's already extended forgiveness.

Paul tells us in Ephesians 5:8–9: "At one time you were darkness, but now you are light in the Lord. Walk as children of the light (for the fruit of light is found in all that is good and right and true)." Truth, not secretiveness or hiding behind a mask of righteousness, is a mark of being a child of light.

Let's face it, if God forgave only the sins we remembered to confess, we would be a hot mess. God still extends forgiveness.

The James 5:16 verse above is particularly applicable to Joseph's brothers. They had admitted their guilt and confessed to Joseph, but not to their father. This half-hearted confession would later come back to pester their consciences after Jacob's death.

In the meantime, Jacob hears Joseph's words from his older sons, sees the wagons of goods, and snaps out of his stupor.

What does Jacob say to his sons in Genesis 45:28?

It is enough. It is enough to know that my child is alive. It is enough to know that I will lay eyes on him once more on this side of heaven. *It is enough.*

Sometimes our journey toward forgiveness, reconciliation, and moving forward in life is arduous. Like Joseph's. Like his older brothers'. Like Jacob's.

From Genesis to Revelation, God faithfully and tirelessly works toward reconciliation between the created and their Creator. Between we who have chosen estrangement and He who chose atonement.

And instead of sacrificing our relationship with Him, Jesus chose to sacrifice His life as our sinless, spotless Passover Lamb who takes away the sin of the world. *Our sin.*

By God's grace, and because of Jesus, we are able to walk as children of the light. So let's walk in it together.

Go Quiet, Go Deep

Quiet your mind from distractions and pull your Bible close. Bow your head and ask Jesus to make His Word and today's lesson personal for you.

Take your time writing out 1 John 1:9.

If you are clinging to an unconfessed sin that is causing you to pull away from God, confess it to Him now and receive the relief of His faithful, cleansing, healing forgiveness.

I pray that the boundless love, grace, and forgiveness of Jesus would penetrate every barrier today so that He can work in you and through you.

WEEK 6

GOD CARES FOR HIS OWN

Genesis 46–47

As Jacob moves his family to Egypt, God visits him in a dream and encourages him not to be afraid. Before Jacob even steps foot in Egypt, God calms his fears by promising to be with him there, as well as promising to return him to the land of His promise. God also speaks another incredible promise over Jacob's life: that He will make Jacob into a great nation. Although Jacob did not live long enough to see that promise come to fruition, Scripture shows that God was indeed faithful once again. Trusting God beyond what we can see is key to walking in His will.

Day 1   Lineage Preserved *(Genesis 46:1–27)*

Day 2   Reunited at Last *(Genesis 46:28–34)*

Day 3   A New Day *(Genesis 47:1–12)*

Day 4   Pharaoh's Steward *(Genesis 47:13–26)*

Day 5   Be Fruitful and Multiply *(Genesis 47:27–31)*

KEY QUESTIONS:

- In what situations do you tend to fear and hesitate to trust God?

- When has God moved you past fear into a wonderful new season or location that would not have taken place had you not trusted Him (such as Joseph being dragged off to Egypt as a slave)?

- How do you become sensitive to God's leading in your life? The key is to remember that He chose us first (see John 15:16).

DAY 1

LINEAGE PRESERVED

So Israel took his journey with all that he had and came to Beer-sheba, and offered sacrifices to the God of his father Isaac. And God spoke to Israel in visions of the night and said, "Jacob, Jacob." And he said, "Here I am." Then he said, "I am God, the God of your father. Do not be afraid to go down to Egypt, for there I will make you into a great nation." (Genesis 46:1–3)

I have lived in Texas my whole life. In fact, I have lived within a one-hundred-mile radius my entire life. However, that radius contains vastly different cultures and priorities.

I grew up near College Station (Aggieland) out in the beautiful countryside with horses and a very simple life. Then we moved to Houston when I was ten and adjusted to the high-level hustle and bustle in the suburbs of America's fourth largest city. Talk about a culture shock! Today, home is near Montgomery, where I again enjoy the peaceful countryside and all those dear to me live not far away.

Even with the drastic cultural change of Houston, several things remained the same regardless of geography: a strong sense of family loyalty and responsibility, Southern manners and hospitality, and Texas pride (if you live outside of Texas, feel free to roll your eyes, but it's kind of a big deal).

I have cheered friends and family who moved across state lines or even internationally, yet I have zero clue what it feels like to live in a completely foreign culture. As an adventurous person, I believe I would wholeheartedly embrace it. At least for a season. But I suspect eventually, like Dorothy in the *Wizard of Oz*, I would feel there's no place like home. The familiar. A place you fit in and don't have to explain why barbecue sauce is part of your DNA.

Jacob and his family have packed their caravan to leave behind the familiar for a serious culture shock. Each mile toward Egypt from Canaan takes them closer to a foreign land with a vastly different culture and priorities, along with a smorgasbord of gods to worship. So, before they reach Egypt, Jacob does something familiar: *worship Yahweh.*

A FAMILIAR PLACE OF WORSHIP

Read Genesis 46:1.

Beersheba is a familiar place of worship for God's people. Located at the southern tip of the Holy Land, Beersheba offers the only remaining fertile land before entering the Negev Desert. Shoring up supplies of water here meant life or death. Two biblical events significant to our study happened at Beersheba. What took place in the following verses?

Genesis 21:25–34

Genesis 26:23–33

Both Jacob's grandfather Abraham and Jacob's father, Isaac, had secured water and worshiped God at Beersheba. Interestingly, Jacob had tricked his brother Esau out of Isaac's blessing at Beersheba and had to flee to Haran (see Genesis 27).

When we trust God and His leading in our lives, He is faithful to turn our former places of shame into renewed places of worship.

How have you seen that true in your own life?

And now Jacob arrives with the third generation of God's people. After they worship and offer sacrifices to God, they settle down for the night.

JACOB'S VISION FROM GOD

Read Genesis 46:2–4. What things does God promise to Jacob in his dream?

Blessings upon blessings! What cool water to Jacob's soul God's words must have felt like despite the famine! Jacob knew right away it was the Lord speaking because it is the third time God had done so with him through dreams or visions. What were the first two times according to the following verses?

Genesis 28:10–17

Genesis 32:22–31

God not only spoke to Jacob in the past—He had wrestled with him so that Jacob walked with a limp from that day until his last. Here, God appears to Jacob specifically to give His approval for Jacob moving his family to Egypt. That is significant because the previous two dreams happened because Jacob was fleeing Esau.

And not only does God give his approval for the move but He also promises, "I Myself will go down with you to Egypt." Just as God was with Joseph in Potiphar's house and prison, so God is with Joseph's father as he journeys to reunite with Joseph.

Still today, God promises to be with you and me as we walk through life's ups and downs. Take time to write out the following verses:

Isaiah 41:10

Matthew 28:20

How do these words affect you in this season of life?

How does God's presence affect your outlook on those circumstances?

It has been an immeasurable blessing to know that God rejoices with me on my happiest days and weeps with me on my saddest days. His loving, watchful presence in our lives makes all the difference. He is Immanuel, God with us, so that we never walk our journey alone.

God also makes another incredible promise to Jacob: "There I will make you into a great nation." Sometimes I think we skip over the word *there* to see the *great nation* part of that verse. *There.* In the place where His people would eventually suffer in terrible bondage, *there* God would make them great.

This reminds me of the spiritual giants in my life whom I look to for godly guidance and counsel. Each of them experienced great suffering over the course of their lives. Yet they will be the first to give God praise for those pain-filled times because they realize it was *there* that God forged in them a strength they would not otherwise have.

Where is your *there*?

How has God strengthened you as a result?

Our *there* may represent a place we would have preferred to skip over at the time. But God has such great work to do within us *there*.

God also promises Jacob: "I will . . . bring you up again." Through Jacob's offspring, God will fulfill this promise in their exodus from Egypt. God never leaves His people, including us, in our *there* without hope.

THE CARAVAN OF GOD'S PEOPLE
Read Genesis 46:5–27.

First, Jacob's sons are listed, followed by the descendants according to their mothers. A total of sixty-six people (see Genesis 46:26). Adding Joseph, his wife, and their two sons brought the number of God's people in Egypt to seventy.

And from that seventy, God formed a great nation that still exists today. Although scattered by geography, God's people cover the globe. And because of Jesus, Gentiles are now among that great number of His people.

It may take many years for God to work in you what He plans to accomplish. It was centuries before God would rescue His people from bondage in a place that had once been a lush oasis in the desert. And yet God promised to make them a great nation *there*. And He promises to be with us through every season, our whole life long.

What God promises *always* comes to pass.

Go Quiet, Go Deep

Quiet your mind from distractions and pull your Bible close. Bow your head and ask Jesus to make His Word and today's lesson personal for you.

Take your time writing out Psalm 23:4.

What does it mean to you personally that God is always walking with you?

I pray that the boundless love, grace, and forgiveness of Jesus would penetrate every barrier today so that He can work in you and through you.

DAY 2

REUNITED AT LAST

Then Joseph prepared his chariot and went up to meet Israel his
father in Goshen. He presented himself to him and fell on his neck
and wept on his neck a good while. Israel said to Joseph, "Now let
me die, since I have seen your face and know that you are still alive."
(Genesis 46:29–30)

On Valentine's Day in 2020, I flew to California to speak at a weekend
event. When the plane landed at LAX, I barely made it into the terminal before encountering a wall of people. They were all talking excitedly and
holding up their cell phone cameras toward those of us who were disembarking.

I stopped and asked the person standing closest to me what they were
waiting for. Holding back tears, she said that her cousin was on that flight.
He had been wounded in Afghanistan and was finally coming home. The
wall of people was his family and friends.

About that time, the disembarking crowd parted, and a soldier appeared
on the gangway supported by crutches with a cast on his right foot. In an
instant, a woman bolted from the crowd, gathered up the soldier in a huge
bear hug, and began to sob uncontrollably. She clung to him, knuckles white,
and would not let go. That soldier was her son.

The whole scene made all of us tear up. We cheered with that family
and took turns thanking that young man for his brave service. When that
soldier had been shipped out, the woman had not expected to see her son
alive again.

That emotional scene provides a snapshot of today's lesson as Jacob finally arrives in Egypt to be reunited with Joseph.

Read Genesis 46:28–29. What stands out to you in these verses?

THE TRANSFORMATION OF JUDAH

At long last, we approach the pinnacle of Joseph's story: the reunion! There is an aspect here that may seem minor but is important to understand.

Which son did Jacob send ahead of their caravan to show the way to Goshen?

Judah was not the oldest among Jacob's sons. However, the Judah we see in this passage has traveled a long road with much trial and tribulation to be transformed by God into such a leader. Let's look at a recap of Judah's life up to this point. What happened in the following verses?

Genesis 38:1–2

Genesis 38:7–10

Genesis 38:24

Genesis 37:26–27

Up to this point, Judah's choices reflect self-centered indulgence. Against God's command, he married a Canaanite woman and became a human trafficker when he took part in selling Joseph as a slave to the Midianites. It is not a compelling résumé, to say the least. But let's face it—are any of us without sin and able to throw stones?

What are some of the less-than-stellar actions you have taken in the past?

When I struggled to make ends meet as a twenty-something in the big city, there were times when I did not have enough money for groceries. Too proud to ask my parents for money, I would head to the grocery store and fill up my basket anyway, knowing that I would intentionally write bad checks to cover the cost. (This was back in the early nineties when people still wrote checks at grocery stores.) And if that wasn't bad enough, I would often write the check for $50 over to receive cash back to purchase gas for my car.

It was only a matter of time before consequences caught up with my choices and the police came knocking on my parents' front door. Thankfully, my dad squared everything away, and I only received a slap on the hand from the court system with no formal charges to haunt me. And even though—by the grace of God alone—I do not have a criminal record, my past reflects some very poor choices.

Judah could say much the same. But when Benjamin was falsely accused of stealing Joseph's silver cup, we see this man whose heart had been convicted and transformed by God come forward to offer his life for Benjamin's freedom. That was pivotal in Judah's walk with the Lord.

By God's grace and through His perfect plan, what did Jesus, the Lion of the tribe of Judah, say in John 10:17–18?

Such hope and unconditional love! God can transform any heart and any life for His glory and our good. No matter how hard we try, we cannot out-sin God's forgiveness.

REUNITED AT LAST

In Genesis 46:29, what was Joseph's reaction upon seeing his father for the first time in twenty years?

Joseph did not greet Jacob with arms-length respect. His emotional reaction demonstrates the deep, genuine affection this son felt for his father. The Hebrew word describing that moment (עוֹד) refers to something that happens repeatedly. Like that woman and her son I saw in the airport, Joseph did not want to let go of his father. White-knuckled, Joseph clings to Jacob as years of hurt, loneliness, and relief flood out through his tears.

How does Jacob respond in Genesis 46:30?

Upon seeing Joseph, Jacob knows that he can depart this life with peace and joy. In other words, *it is enough*. There is nothing else in life that Jacob desires. No wealth, fame, accolades, possessions, or friendships. *This is enough.* As you and I strive toward various markers through life, our actions say that we have yet to reach that point. After high school, we strive for college. After college, a job. A spouse. Perhaps children. A house and a new car. Then financial stability. Perhaps travel. And retirement. Then what?

Have you reached "it is enough" in your life? If not, what are you still striving for?

I believe I will reach that point in my personal life, but never in ministry. There is always another heart to reach for Jesus, another hand to hold, and a downcast fellow warrior to encourage. In Jesus, we have enough. In serving Him, there is always more to do. However, for Jacob at that moment, he experiences *enough*. What a beautiful place to rest.

JOSEPH PAVES THE WAY WITH PHARAOH

Read Genesis 46:31–34.

Out of an abundance of caution (probably taking into account his brothers' former careless actions), Joseph carefully explains to his family what will happen (and how they will need to respond) as they stand before Pharaoh.

Although this exchange may seem odd, these verses provide insight into why Joseph was such a highly valued administrator. Yes, God blessed all he did, but Joseph's cautious diligence routinely ensured that every situation received careful thought and precise execution.

SHEPHERDS, AN ABOMINATION?

What is the last phrase of Genesis 46:34?

This is an interesting twist because in the New Testament, it is usually the Jews who will not share table fellowship for reasons of ritual cleanliness. However, earlier in Joseph's narrative, we learned that this was not the first time that Egyptians would not eat with Hebrews (see Genesis 43:32).

Jewish scholars have noted that such an aversion did not initially exist in Egypt until Upper Egypt and Lower Egypt became unified. After that time, a sense of puritanism seeped into the culture over the years. By the time Joseph arrived, Egypt's puritan rituals had been adopted as a way of life.[13]

So, after twenty years of grieving the separation from his family, Joseph diligently prepares them to go before Pharaoh. A new season of blessing awaits. God will bless Jacob and Joseph with a life of plenty instead of famine for the rest of their days.

And in that moment, *it was enough.*

Go Quiet, Go Deep

Quiet your mind from distractions and pull your Bible close. Bow your head and ask Jesus to make His Word and today's lesson personal for you.

Take your time writing out Philippians 4:11–12.

What does it mean to you personally to live content in the Lord?

I pray that the boundless love, grace, and forgiveness of Jesus would penetrate every barrier today so that He can work in you and through you.

DAY 3

A NEW DAY

So Joseph went in and told Pharaoh, "My father and my brothers, with their flocks and herds and all that they possess, have come from the land of Canaan. They are now in the land of Goshen." (Genesis 47:1)

When I began attending church in October 1990, I remember feeling nervous to tell my family. Even though mom and dad had been raised in church as children, it was not the routine in our home when I was growing up. We were Christmas and Easter church attenders, but I had never been baptized.

Then, after a few months of faithfully attending church (which was a surprise in and of itself), God made it very clear through the Bible classes, sermons, and devotions at home that He had been the missing element in my life all along. God had stirred faith in my heart, and I wanted to be baptized. I approached my senior pastor and asked him what I needed to do to be baptized and become a member of Salem (where I still belong more than thirty years later).

He was ecstatic and walked me through what would need to be done. We set a date for my Baptism to take place soon. Then he asked me if he could baptize me *during* the church service instead of before or after it. He said that such a beautiful act of faith as a young adult would be a wonderful encouragement to the congregation. *Gulp.*

I was nervous on many levels. I asked my mom, dad, and sisters to come to Salem on the day of my Baptism. They happily agreed. Yet I was still nervous. The church—like Jesus—had lovingly accepted and embraced me as I was. *But would they accept and embrace my family?*

My family means the world to me. As the old saying goes, "I can pick on my family, but nobody else better do it." This was very true for me. But it went deeper. I believed that if my church would accept my family, then so would God. I realize such a thought is way off base, but as a fledgling believer, it was an honest one.

When all was said and done, my baptismal day was absolutely beautiful in every way. God welcomed me into His forever family, and my family was welcomed by my new church family.

As we open to Genesis 47, we find Joseph in a similar position. After faithfully serving Pharaoh for almost a decade, it's time for Joseph to introduce his family to the most powerful ruler on earth. Would everything go well?

STANDING BEFORE PHARAOH
Read Genesis 47:1–6. What stands out to you in these verses?

After his family arrived, Joseph appears before Pharaoh to respectfully let him know that all has happened as Pharaoh had graciously granted.

What does Genesis 47:2 tell us?

Joseph had eleven brothers but brought only five before Pharaoh. We do not know which ones Joseph chose, but it would likely be those men who understood in some capacity how to behave in a royal court (or perhaps even had experience). Joseph finally had his family around him again, and he was not going to let anything jeopardize it.

Have you ever been in a similar situation? If so, what happened?

Pharaoh asks the questions that Joseph told his brothers would be asked. And they answer as Joseph had instructed them. However, there is an important word usage we need to note. It provides a comparison that reveals how the brothers view their time in Goshen versus how Pharoah views it.

Fill in the blank from Genesis 47:4:

"We have come to _____ in the land."

The Hebrew word *sojourn* that the brothers use (רוּג) means to dwell for a time. It's a word that references a more indefinite or temporary timeframe. God had promised long ago that Egypt would never be His people's permanent home.

When Pharoah addresses the brothers in Genesis 47:6, he tells them, "*Settle* your father and your brothers in the best of the land." The Hebrew *settle* (בְּשֵׁי) means to sit, remain, or abide. It is a word that carries the meaning of setting up a home or to marry. In other words, they would be there for the long haul.

As God's children, you and I are sojourners on earth. This is not our permanent home. The victory that Christ won on the cross on our behalf secured our permanent home in heaven.

What does Ephesians 2:19 tell us?

We are strangers here, just as Joseph and his family were strangers in Egypt. Our home is rooted in the eternal.

How does that perspective change or confirm the way you think about our time on Earth?

Jacob before Pharaoh
Read Genesis 47:7–10.

Joseph brings Jacob before Pharaoh, and Jacob is given the opportunity to bless Pharoah. At 130 years old, just think of how much wisdom Jacob could share about life, faith, and trusting God.

Although Jacob's blessing is not recorded in Scripture, the mere fact that Jacob took that step is convicting when we become shy about sharing the love and blessings of God with others.

Jacob could have easily been intimidated to stand in front of Pharaoh, who led one of the most powerful nations on earth at the time. But his relationship to Joseph drove away all fears.

Write 1 John 4:18.

Sometimes we get so caught in what we lack—experience, knowledge, compassion, money, or position—that we fear failure. Failure that we will not meet the needs of others. Failure that they will not meet ours. When you and I are intimidated about speaking to others about our faith, our relationship with Jesus can drive away all our fears.

GETTING SETTLED IN GOSHEN
Read Genesis 47:11–12.

Finally, after more than two decades, Joseph and his family are reunited and will be blessed to spend the rest of their lives involved in one another's lives. Joseph's father and brothers would finally get to meet Joseph's wife and two sons.

One of God's greatest blessings in my life is to have my mom and sisters all live no more than fifteen minutes away. There are many impromptu dinners, informal events, birthday parties, and big holiday celebrations.

Through today's lesson, we have been blessed to see how God can heal family estrangement—even one that included attempted murder, slavery, betrayal, half-truths, and self-centered behavior.

If your family struggles with estrangement, know that God is pro-family, pro-love, and pro-forgiveness. Nothing is impossible with God.

Go Quiet, Go Deep

Quiet your mind from distractions and pull your Bible close. Bow your head and ask Jesus to make His Word and today's lesson personal for you.

Take your time writing out Psalm 46:1–3.

What does it mean to you personally that God will remove fear when you take refuge in Him?

I pray that the boundless love, grace, and forgiveness of Jesus would penetrate every barrier today so that He can work in you and through you.

DAY 4

PHARAOH'S STEWARD

Now there was no food in all the land, for the famine was very severe, so that the land of Egypt and the land of Canaan languished by reason of the famine. And Joseph gathered up all the money that was found in the land of Egypt and in the land of Canaan, in exchange for the grain that they bought. And Joseph brought the money into Pharaoh's house. (Genesis 47:13–14)

During World War II, the U.S. federal government instituted a rationing system to conserve certain high-demand goods. This mandatory system ensured that troops and citizens alike would have enough food and crucial supplies. At the top of the rationing list were food, shoes, metal, paper, and rubber.

According to the National WWII Museum in New Orleans, Louisiana, the rationing system worked like this:

> The government issued a number of "points" to each person, even babies, which had to be turned in along with money to purchase goods made with restricted items. In 1943 for example, a pound of bacon cost about 30 cents, but a shopper would also have to turn in seven ration points to buy the meat. These points came in the form of stamps that were distributed to citizens in books throughout the war.[14]

Because of the war effort, automobile tires were the first item to be rationed a week after Pearl Harbor was attacked. Automobile makers converted their production facilities to crank out military trucks, ambulances, and tanks instead of personal automobiles. The first food item to be rationed was sugar, followed by coffee (*gasp!*), meats, cheeses, canned fish, and milk.

Communities rallied to plant victory gardens, growing vegetables to both consume and share. Newspapers and other sources regularly provided endless tips on ways that families could enjoy balanced meals while maximizing use of their ration points. It truly was a nationwide effort to survive.

The rationing system effectively prevented hoarding so that everyone had a chance to obtain basic supplies to survive. Following our recent global pandemic and subsequent inflation of basic food and supplies, we can certainly appreciate WWII's rationing system a little more. I certainly do.

Several times throughout Joseph's narrative, we get a glimpse at the extraordinary administrative gifts God bestowed on him. When Joseph ran Potiphar's home, God gave him success. When Joseph ran the prison in which he was incarcerated, God gave him success. And all because the Lord was with him.

Now, as the famine turns severe, we are given an even greater view of how Joseph wielded his God-given and Pharaoh-granted power so people would have enough to survive.

Read Genesis 47:13–22. What stands out to you in these verses?

THE FAMINE STILL RAGES

In Joseph's narrative, we have reached Egypt's third year of famine. We cannot properly picture what that even looked like. When food supplies diminish, the first casualties are the livestock. Then the livestock becomes the food supply. But what happens after the livestock is gone? You can see how quickly a famine could devastate any land.

From 1983 to 1985, we saw this firsthand as Ethiopia experienced a famine that historians agree was the worst humanitarian event of the twentieth century. In fact, one British reporter called it a "biblical famine in the 20th century."[15] Ethiopia's famine resulted in approximately one million deaths with millions of others displaced without resources to rebuild.

One million people lost their lives by the time Ethiopia experienced its third year of famine. Egypt and Canaan now enter their third year of famine. The situation is grave. But God had prepared and moved Joseph into the position of Egypt's prime minister to provide hope and relief amid desperation.

JOSEPH GATHERS MONEY
In Genesis 47:13–14, what does Joseph gather?

When it comes to money, one truth is universal: you can't eat it. Regardless of any Egyptian's status, food was necessary. Granted, the wealthy were likely able to buy Joseph's grain for a longer period of time than others, but these verses tell us that *all* of the money had been gathered.

Now 100 percent of the people have depleted their financial resources and become dependent on Pharaoh's storehouses to survive the famine. So why didn't Joseph just give the hungry people grain? *The Lutheran Study Bible* says, "[Joseph] preferred to sell the corn rather than give it to the hungry . . . lest if they received it for nothing, they should give up cultivating the ground. . . . He did not wish to deprive all of them of their property, but to support them in it."[16]

Here we can insert the old Chinese proverb about teaching a man to fish and he will be fed for a lifetime.

What does 2 Thessalonians 3:10 tell us?

Joseph realized that it was beneficial to encourage people to maintain good stewardship of their resources rather than create lifelong beggars well after the famine ended.

JOSEPH GATHERS LIVESTOCK
In Genesis 47:15–17, what does Joseph gather?

Pharaoh now had all of Egypt's money, horses, flocks, herds, and donkeys.

At the very end of verse 17, an important phrase jumps off the page: *that year*. This points to the likelihood that Joseph gave a fair price for their live-stock. For the herds to provide a whole year's worth of grain, price-gouging was not part of Joseph's plan.

It is important to remember here that, through the dreams that Joseph interpreted for Pharaoh, Joseph knows that famine will eventually end. This catastrophe is not the end of the world. Joseph works in such a way as to retain and maintain the people's trust long after the famine ends.

JOSEPH GATHERS LAND AND PEOPLE
In Genesis 47:18–22, what does Joseph gather?

At first glance, we may be inclined to think that Joseph has become a heartless tyrant. He made the people purchase grain until their money ran out. Then he made them barter away all of their livestock for grain. Now, has he become a human trafficker like his brothers were?

Joseph is acting as an able fiscal steward for Pharaoh. The people still had resources for which to obtain grain, so Joseph bartered accordingly.

Do you find it comfortable to ask people to help you with basic needs such as food or money? Why or why not?

By purchasing and bartering with the people for grain, Joseph demonstrates that he understood the importance of a person's self-worth. Very few of us like to be beggars.

According to Ephesians 2:10, what is your worth to God?

You are a breathtaking piece of workmanship made by the Master Craftsman. A beautiful display of God's holy creativity and perfect skills. One of a kind. If you are feeling "less than" today, remember this: your worth is based on His worth and workmanship.

Bought for a Price

Read Genesis 47:23–26.

Joseph has now bought and acquired for Pharaoh all of Egypt's money, land, livestock, and people. Had it been our contemporary culture, we might have shouted at the unfairness. Shouted that Joseph took advantage of the people. Complained to Pharaoh until Joseph lost his position or his life. But that's not what happened.

What do the people say in Genesis 47:25?

You have saved our lives. They had been bought for a price and gained life. So they willingly served Joseph in the fields. Because of Joseph's diligence and watchful care, they were going to make it.

What does 1 Corinthians 6:20 tell us?

Jesus values you so highly that He bought you for a price. His life was the price. In Him, we gained eternal life. So we willingly serve Him in the harvest fields. And because of Jesus' great love for us, we are going to make it out of this world alive for all eternity. Thank You, Jesus!

Go Quiet, Go Deep

Quiet your mind from distractions and pull your Bible close. Bow your head and ask Jesus to make His Word and today's lesson personal for you.

Take your time writing out 1 Corinthians 6:20.

What does it mean to you personally that Jesus values you so highly, He bought you with His life to rescue you from eternal famine?

I pray that the boundless love, grace, and forgiveness of Jesus would penetrate every barrier today so that He can work in you and through you.

DAY 5

BE FRUITFUL AND MULTIPLY

Thus Israel settled in the land of Egypt, in the land of Goshen. And they gained possessions in it, and were fruitful and multiplied greatly. (Genesis 47:27)

It was a blustery, chilly evening in the fall of 2000, and I still remember where I was standing when my dad called. I had just cleaned up the kitchen after dinner and was getting ready to relax in the living room and watch some television.

I jumped up when the phone rang (it was a landline in the kitchen) and answered with a cheery greeting. The second I heard Dad's voice, I knew something was wrong. Mom was usually the one who called to chit-chat. Dad preferred in-person chats. Even so, he didn't sound okay.

I asked him if anything was wrong, and he simply said, "Is there a place you can sit down, honey?" I sank to the kitchen floor and repeated my question. He said, "Well, honey, the doctors say that I have cancer."

I don't remember much of what he said after that. I just started crying. He attempted all kinds of soothing explanations and promising treatment results, but I knew. This bona fide daddy's girl just knew. And I could tell from his voice that he did too. *At that moment, time became a very precious commodity.*

As I stood listening to the 21-gun salute at Dad's funeral on May 2, 2003, I remembered that phone call. We both knew then that this day would arrive all too soon. And even though I drove from Houston to Fort Worth every other weekend during that two and a half years, I wish we'd had more time.

If you have ever been in a similar situation, you know that time both speeds up and stops completely. At this point in Genesis, we see that after living in Egypt for seventeen years, Joseph's elderly father begins to fade.

BE FRUITFUL AND MULTIPLY
Read Genesis 47:27–31. What stands out to you in these verses?

As Egypt's famine worsens all around them, Jacob and his family flourish in Goshen. They not only gain possessions but also witness God's promise become a reality.

In Genesis 46:3, what did God promise Jacob in his dream?

As his son Joseph had seen his prophetic dreams come to fruition, Jacob now sees his prophetic dream come to life before his eyes. However, this is not the first time that Scripture references that His people will be fruitful and multiply. In what context do you see it in the following verses?

Genesis 1:27–28

Genesis 9:1

There are two implications in the phrase, "be fruitful and multiply." The first is to multiply as human beings as we see with Adam and Eve and again with Noah. The second is to multiply as the Church as we see in the Book of Acts. As the disciples traveled far and wide to spread the Gospel, the Church multiplied and was fruitful. Look up and write down the following verses:

Romans 10:1

John 15:16

When the Church follows God's will, we see Acts 6:7 become a reality with our own eyes: "And the word of God continued to increase, and the number of the disciples multiplied greatly in Jerusalem." Jacob was blessed, indeed, to see the long-standing promise of God continue to be fulfilled in his own generation.

How have you seen that particular promise of God be fulfilled in your own church or circles of influence?

JOSEPH'S PROMISE

Jacob has now reached 147 years old and his earthly clock begins to tick louder. So he calls Joseph to his side.

What does Jacob ask of Joseph in Genesis 47:29–30?

There is something comforting about knowing where our earthly bones will rest. Since my dad had served in the Air Force, he wanted to be laid to rest in Houston's National Cemetery. Mom will be laid to rest directly above him in the same plot. Military cemeteries allow the spouses of military service men and women to be buried together with the service member. Knowing Mom's wishes, Dad was buried at a depth of nine feet. Mom will rest directly above him at a depth of six feet, and her name will be added to Dad's existing military marker.

Jacob seeks from Joseph the comfort of knowing where he will be laid to rest. Although Jacob lived in Egypt, he never forgot Canaan, so he asks to be buried with his fathers in their "burying place." This beautifully expresses Jacob's faith in God's promises—the land, a great nation, but most of all, the Savior that would come from their descendants.

According to Genesis 23:17–20, where is the burying place of Jacob's ancestors?

Who is buried there, according to Genesis 25:7–11?

Eventually, Isaac, Rebekah, and Leah would join Abraham, Sarah, and Jacob in the cave of Machpelah (see Genesis 49:29–32). The cave is still there today, and a large mosque has been built over it (in a similar manner to how churches that Christians have built sit over many of our holy sites in Israel). Both Jews and Muslims hold the cave of Machpelah as a sacred site.

Jacob Makes an Oath with Joseph

With his hand under his father's thigh, Joseph swears to Jacob that he will be buried in the burying place that his father requested. (Placing a hand under someone's thigh was simply a cultural gesture that accompanied oaths.)

What is the last sentence of Genesis 47:31?

This is not the moment where Jacob (Israel) dies, but it likely means that he was weary and could no longer sit up straight. At 147 years old, and living a nomadic lifestyle until settling in Goshen, he was entitled to be weary.

I have spoken with many Christians over the years who have said that they are afraid of death. While I must admit that wondering *how* I will die might cause me to pause, death itself means the beginning of forever with Jesus.

He who crushed the serpent's head. He who took your nails. He who gave His life for yours. He who redeemed you from hell.

On that day, you will finally be able to look straight into your Savior's eyes and see an all-consuming love reflected there. *For you.*

Death is merely the gateway to experiencing that incredible moment.

Go Quiet, Go Deep

Quiet your mind from distractions and pull your Bible close. Bow your head and ask Jesus to make His Word and today's lesson personal for you.

Take your time writing out Isaiah 54:10.

What does it mean to you personally that God's love for you will never fail?

I pray that the boundless love, grace, and forgiveness of Jesus would penetrate every barrier today so that He can work in you and through you.

WEEK 7

EMBRACING GOD'S BLESSINGS

Genesis 48:1–49:27

As Jacob nears the end of his life, Joseph comes to his side. Again, Jacob passes over the older brothers to single out Joseph for a special blessing. But God does not begrudge him for it. Joseph brings his sons, Ephraim and Manasseh, to receive their grandfather's blessing. This seems foreign in our culture today, but what a powerful impact it would have on future generations. The blessing of a loving, supportive family can never be taken for granted. And the ultimate giver of those blessings can never be overlooked to receive our thankfulness and gratitude.

DAY 1   Remembering God's Faithfulness (*Genesis 48:1–7*)

DAY 2   Receiving God's Blessings (*Genesis 48:8–22*)

DAY 3   Prophetic Blessings for Reuben, Simeon, and Levi (*Genesis 49:1–7*)

DAY 4   Prophetic Blessing Over the Tribe of Judah (*Genesis 49:8–12*)

DAY 5   Prophetic Blessings for Jacob's Remaining Sons (*Genesis 49:13–27*)

KEY QUESTIONS:

- When someone speaks a blessing over you, do you embrace it or question it?

- If you are a parent, have you ever specifically blessed your child(ren) in a personal, meaningful way?

- Did you ever receive a blessing from a grandparent? If so, what have you seen come about in your life as a result?

DAY 1

REMEMBERING GOD'S FAITHFULNESS

And Jacob said to Joseph, "God Almighty appeared to me at Luz in the land of Canaan and blessed me, and said to me, 'Behold, I will make you fruitful and multiply you, and I will make of you a company of peoples and will give this land to your offspring after you for an everlasting possession.'" (Genesis 48:3–4)

At 147 years old, Jacob prepares for his final days on earth. His life has been riddled with great blessing and favor from God, along with great sadness and family turmoil.

Among other significant milestones, Jacob had four wives, twelve sons, andat least a couple of daughters; wrestled with God and lived; received God's generational blessing and promise; allowed favoritism to create a rift among his sons for more than two decades; and eventually reunited with his long-lost son, Joseph, who had become prime minister of Egypt and saved God's people from perishing in the famine.

And those are just the highlights. And now the time has come for Jacob to pass along God's blessings to the next generation of leaders.

JOSEPH TAKES HIS SONS TO JACOB
Read Genesis 48:1–2. What stands out to you in these verses?

Joseph receives word that his father is ill and rushes to his father's side. The Hebrew word used regarding the level of Jacob's illness, *chalah* (חָלָה), specifically refers to an illness from which Jacob would die in this context.

In 2 Kings 13:14, the same reference is used regarding what person?

Elisha had lived a long life after receiving a prophetic blessing from Elijah. Where Jacob had been his father's son and received a prophetic, generational blessing, Elisha had been a disciple and protégé of Elijah and received a prophetic, double portion of Elijah's power.

In both circumstances, we are shown the God-given power of prophetic blessings. When Joseph rushes to his father's side, he brings his two sons, Manasseh and Ephraim, with him so as not to miss the opportunity.

Jacob Recalls God's Faithfulness
Read Genesis 48:3–7.

If you spend much time around elderly people, you know what great storytellers they can be. They talk about days long before we were born and how much things have changed during their lifetime. Younger people sometimes become impatient with all the stories. But our impatience means we may miss out not just on a story but a spiritual blessing as well.

Older adults are able to look in the rearview mirror of their lives to see the trail of God's faithfulness. Hearing those stories provides uplifting assurance for the next generation that God never leaves nor forsakes us. Write out the following verses for your own assurance today:

Deuteronomy 31:6–8

Joshua 1:9

Jacob prefaces his blessing by retelling the blessing of God's faithfulness. Because of His faithfulness, Jesus gave His life so that we would inherit His eternal blessings.

Prophetic Blessings

We saw previously in this study that Jacob had stolen the blessing of his brother, Esau, from their father, Isaac. Jacob was not the older son, so the firstborn's birthright and blessing should have gone to Esau.

Here we see a similar situation, except this time Joseph did not use trickery. Joseph was not the oldest son of his father, Jacob, so the firstborn blessing privileges should have gone to Reuben's sons instead of Joseph's sons. However, Jacob chooses to pass the blessing to Joseph.

What does Jacob say to Joseph in Genesis 48:5?

Jacob adopts Manasseh and Ephraim as his own and, in doing so, gives Joseph's line a double portion of future land in Canaan. Joseph would not be one of the twelve tribes of Israel, but *both* of his sons who were born in Egypt would be.

Since the tribe of Levi (the Levites) would be landless as God's priestly tribe, the land of Canaan would still be divided into twelve parts because of Joseph's double portion through Manasseh and Ephraim.

JACOB RECALLS HIS GREATEST HEARTACHE
What does Jacob tell Joseph in Genesis 48:7?

If you have been around anyone who has very little time left on earth, they often express their greatest sorrow or regrets. And Jacob is no different as he recalls his greatest earthly love with lingering grief. What a beautiful blessing in that moment for Joseph to hear that his mom and dad shared a great love, even though their time together had been cut short.

For children to witness genuine love and affection between their parents is one of the greatest blessings that any parent can pass along to the next generation. It provides a deep sense of security for children to know that even though mom and dad may argue or not always agree, they are still committed to facing the world together as one.

Of course, not everyone has experienced such a blessing in their childhood, whether as a result of divorce or death or other circumstances.

However, we can still demonstrate that such love is possible by the way we foster a loving family environment as a whole.

A Window of Grace

Sometimes God gifts us with a window of time before a parent departs this life. Joseph experienced both the unexpected, sudden loss of his mother and the window of grace with his father before Jacob passed away.

Have you experienced such a window of grace with one of your parents? If so, what was the greatest blessing from God as a result?

I experienced that window of grace with my dad. The meaningful conversations. The intentionality to live in the moment since we did not know how many moments were left. And the opportunity for me to thank him for being absolutely the best dad in the whole world.

Because God had faithfully orchestrated their reunion in Egypt, God blessed Joseph with that window of grace with his dad.

What a beautiful truth it is to know that our window of grace with our heavenly Father will last for all eternity.

Go Quiet, Go Deep

Quiet your mind from distractions and pull your Bible close. Bow your head and ask Jesus to make His Word and today's lesson personal for you.

Take your time writing out Ephesians 5:15–16a.

What does it mean to you personally to make the best use of your time?

I pray that the boundless love, grace, and forgiveness of Jesus would penetrate every barrier today so that He can work in you and through you.

DAY 2

RECEIVING GOD'S BLESSINGS

When Israel saw Joseph's sons, he said, "Who are these?" Joseph said to this father, "They are my sons, whom God has given me here." And he said, "Bring them to me, please, that I may bless them." (Genesis 48:8–9)

I had never heard of family or generational blessings until I started reading the Bible in my twenties. It was not something I was familiar with in the least. The closest I ever came to experiencing any kind of formal blessing happened at my adult confirmation. Receiving my pastor's blessing to faithfully love and serve God wholeheartedly felt both empowering and sobering in equal measure.

I believe that, at age 23, I understood on a much deeper level what being confirmed into the faith means than if I had been confirmed earlier in my life. Now, almost three decades later, I have experienced God bringing that blessing to fruition as He empowers me to serve Him in this ministry with sober responsibility and joy-filled passion.

Other than a general pastoral blessing following Communion or a pastor reciting Aaron's blessing over the congregation at the end of a church service, has someone ever formally spoken a blessing over your life? If so, how have you seen God working to bring it to fruition?

Learning about the significance of various blessings that occur in Scripture has been a fascinating journey, to say the least. Significant meaning lies behind not only who receives the blessings but the order in which they receive them.

BLESSINGS IN SCRIPTURE

Before we dive into today's text, it is important to understand how blessings worked in biblical times and what they accomplished. Blessings were such an integral part of Old Testament times that various versions of the word *blessing* occur hundreds of times.

First, a blessing was a public declaration of God's favor upon a person's life. And second, the blessing imparted power for success and prosperity. Blessings also served as a guide and pathway for a person's life. All of the patriarchs (Abraham, Isaac, and Jacob) gave formal blessings to their children. In Jacob's case alone, he was also able to bless two grandchildren.

God also spoke covenant blessings over the nation of Israel as His chosen people. How do you see God's blessings in the following verses?

Numbers 6:24–26

Deuteronomy 28:1–14

JACOB'S BLESSINGS

Read Genesis 48:8–22. What stands out to you in these verses?

At 147 years old, Jacob has difficulty identifying his grandsons. However, "dim with age" simply means old age. Jacob's eyesight may have been dim, but the blessings God inspired him to pass along to Manasseh and Ephraim were anything but dim. Even though they had been born in Egypt, Jacob adopts his two grandsons into the people of God. By doing so, he made it possible for them to receive the inheritance of the Lord.

It is easy to make that concept personal for us. Chances are you, like me, were born in America to Gentile parents, yet God graciously adopted us at our Baptism into His forever family (see Galatians 3:27–4:7). As His children, we will receive the inheritance of the Lord.

Before Jacob begins speaking his blessings, what does he say in Genesis 48:11?

After seventeen years in Egypt, Jacob still cannot comprehend the beautiful blessing of God allowing him to be reunited with his favorite son. And since God loves to bless us outrageously, Jacob was also able to see Joseph's offspring. Perhaps glimpse traces of Joseph's face reflected in Manasseh and Ephraim. That is a special gift that God gives to grandparents.

By now, Joseph had been the second-highest official in Egypt for well over two decades, yet he still remembers the honor and reverence due to his father in their patriarchal society. As he hands over Manasseh and Ephraim to receive their blessings, Joseph bows low before his father (see Genesis 48:12). This is yet another unspoken blessing received by Manasseh and Ephraim; their father's behavior teaches them proper respect for their elders.

MANASSEH'S AND EPHRAIM'S BLESSING

Manasseh and Ephraim are grown men by the time Jacob blesses them. Even though their exact ages are unknown and scholars vary in their conclusions, Manasseh and Ephraim were at least in their twenties (if not older) by the time Jacob blessed them.

Joseph takes both sons to Jacob and places them in the proper places to receive their blessings.

In Genesis 48:13, how did Joseph position his sons?

In Genesis 48:14, what did Jacob do?

The hands that Jacob chose to bless each grandson with were used with a specific purpose. In Scripture, the right had was the favored position since it is associated with God's strength (see Exodus 15:6). That is the reason that Jesus took His seat in heaven at the right hand of God the Father (see Mark 14:62).

Even though Genesis 48:15 starts out, "And he blessed Joseph," Jacob did not physically bless Joseph at that point. Rather, by blessing Joseph's sons, Joseph was also blessed. If you are a parent, you have probably experienced that feeling of blessing to see your children receive a blessing in some way or another.

So, with Jacob's right hand on Ephraim's head and his left on Manasseh's, Jacob blessed both grandsons.

Read Genesis 48:15–16 once more. What elements are contained in Jacob's blessing?

Jacob displays deep awareness that God made a covenant with both Abraham and Isaac and that God has faithfully shepherded and provided for His people through them. And like the patriarchs before him, Jacob passes along the blessing for Ephraim and Manasseh to be fruitful and multiply.

Joseph is upset when he notices that his father has crossed his hands and, consequently, the blessing. Joseph tries to correct Jacob, but Jacob knew that the blessings were given as God had intended.

What explanation does Jacob give Joseph in Genesis 48:19?

In God's economy, firstborn does not necessarily mean first out of the womb. Rather, it is first in order of preeminence. We see that truth in King David's life as well. Even though he was the youngest son, God elevated David to the position of firstborn (see 1 Samuel 16:11; Psalm 89:27).

Jacob affirms that Ephraim, born second, will be greater than Manasseh, the firstborn. This is a fascinating parallel to Jacob himself, whom God chose to be preeminent over his older twin brother (see Genesis 25:23).

What does Jeremiah 31:9 say about Ephraim?

Jacob could have chosen to bless his grandsons how he saw best, yet he followed God's leading, and the blessings came to fruition.

GOD'S BLESSINGS UPON YOU

Whether person to person or God to His people, blessings for those who love the Lord are woven throughout the Bible. In the following verses, what are some of the blessings He has made to you as His beloved child?

Ephesians 1:3–8

As you have time, I encourage you to search Scripture to discover all of the blessings that He has given you as a faithful follower of Jesus.

God loves us so much that His blessings would literally take pages and pages to write out.

Go Quiet, Go Deep

Quiet your mind from distractions and pull your Bible close. Bow your head and ask Jesus to make His Word and today's lesson personal for you.

Take your time writing out Luke 11:28.

What does it mean to you personally that you will be blessed when you hear and keep God's Word?

I pray that the boundless love, grace, and forgiveness of Jesus would penetrate every barrier today so that He can work in you and through you.

DAY 3

Prophetic Blessings
for Reuben, Simeon, and Levi

> Then Jacob called his sons and said, "Gather yourselves together, that I may tell you what shall happen to you in days to come." (Genesis 49:1)

Many people say that growing up as a middle child was a trying experience for them. Psychologists and mental health experts have come up with long lists delineating the traits and challenges of middle children. However, as a middle child, I highly recommend it.

I have one sister who is four years older than me and two younger sisters with three years between each of us. Looking back on our childhood, I believe that being the second oldest was the prime spot. I would push all the blame for any trouble that I caused up the ladder to my older sister "who should have been watching me better." Then, I wheedled to delegate all my chores down the ladder to my two younger sisters "who just played all the time." Charming, right?

Of course, neither was true but mom and dad often bought it. Perhaps I got away with it because I looked so angelic with blonde curls and blue eyes in contrast to my sisters' dark hair and brown or hazel eyes. I know that's just wrong, but there it is. Feel free to call me a brat.

In America, a child's birth order is not usually a life-changing element in family dynamics. Though it may provide some small perks or challenges of being the oldest or youngest, children are generally treated equally when it comes to inheritance.

In biblical times, however, birth order carried much significance. The *primogeniture*, meaning the firstborn son of the same father, was given exclusive rights of inheritance. Specifically, the firstborn son received a double portion of his father's inheritance. In addition, it was custom for the firstborn son to assume all of his father's authority if the father died or was absent for an extended period of time.

When a father bestowed his birthright, it brought honor and status to the son who received it. A birthright could be sold as well, which we have seen between Jacob and Esau (see Genesis 25:29–34).

And, as we studied on Day 2, paternal blessings carried much significance. Jacob was well aware of this and conspired with his mother to steal Esau's blessing from their father (see Genesis 27:36).

Now, as Jacob's life draws to an end, it is time for him to bestow his blessings on his twelve sons. In our modern day, we would call it a verbal last will and testament. By birth order, the firstborn blessing should have gone to Reuben. But God had other plans.

REUBEN'S BLESSING

Read Genesis 49:1–4. What stands out to you in these verses?

Like a sunny day interrupted by a thunderstorm, Reuben's blessing starts off well and then turns into an indictment of his sin.

What does Jacob say in Genesis 49:4?

To understand Jacob's reference, we need to go back a bit. Reuben, Jacob's firstborn, had the right of the head of the family and the double portion of his father's inheritance. But Reuben had messed up along the way.

What happened in Genesis 35:22?

Because of Reuben's adultery with Rachel's maidservant Bilhah, he lost both rights. Today, his actions would be tantamount to sleeping with his father's girlfriend. No reason is given for why Reuben chose to commit such a sin against Jacob. However, immediately preceding Reuben's actions, Jacob had lost Rachel during Benjamin's birth (see Genesis 35:16–22). Reuben's mother, Leah, had been given to Jacob through deceit (see Genesis 29:21–25), and Jacob never loved Leah as he did Rachel (see Genesis 29:30). Perhaps watching his father give lukewarm love to his mother had rubbed Reuben the wrong way. What better way to get back at your dad than to physically demonstrate lukewarm love toward his concubine? We can only speculate.

Now, all these years later, Jacob still grieves over Reuben's actions. The result is that Jacob pronounces a curse over Reuben by taking away his first-born rights and privileges.

The curse over Reuben's tribe is a reminder to us of the ruinous consequences that come about when we fail to control our desires.

According to Isaiah 59:2a, what is one of the consequences when we sin?

Every single sin is an abomination to God, but the resulting separation from Him is by far the biggest consequence. This is why confession and repentance are integral parts of a believer's life. Through them, God restores us to Himself from that separation.

Jacob's reference to Reuben as "unstable as water" is particularly telling because water can either sustain life or destroy it. Living on the Texas Gulf Coast and having endured many hurricanes over the years, I can attest firsthand that "unstable water" can cause catastrophic destruction.

But instead of disowning or disinheriting Reuben because of that sin, Jacob basically downgrades Reuben's prominence and influence. Even though he forfeited his firstborn rights, Reuben still receives a blessing and becomes head of the one of the twelve tribes.

SIMEON'S AND LEVI'S BLESSINGS
Read Genesis 49:5–7. What stands out to you in these verses?

Wow! Those are fierce words from Jacob, indeed. Simeon and Levi are

Jacob's second and third sons, respectively. Again, to understand Jacob's words, we need to look back.

What happened to their sister Dinah in Genesis 34:1–2?

After Jacob did not hold the perpetrators accountable, what did Simeon and Levi do in Genesis 34:25–29?

Simeon and Levi took it upon themselves to avenge their sister Dinah's rape. Their extreme fury and revenge upon her attacker *and* every man in the neighboring village *and* plundering the village was a sinful stench to Jacob and the inhabitants of the land (see Genesis 34:30). Although their motive to defend Dinah's honor was honorable, their actions were not.

Over time, Simeon's tribe was scattered to a territory far west of the Dead Sea. However, we see God's grace and providence regarding the tribe of Levi. The Levites became God's priestly line who were responsible for all of the priestly duties, including the care of the Old Testament tabernacle and ark of the covenant.

Even when we commit egregious sins, we are never outside of the redemptive love and grace of God. And in the case of Levi's tribe, they were not only redeemed but selected by God to care for His earthly tabernacle and other priestly responsibilities for the rest of their lives.

OUR TAKEAWAY

One of the countless advantages of being able to hold Scripture in our hands is the window it provides to see the purposes of God. Although it is certainly a blessing to glimpse God's thought process, understanding His purposes behind His actions fosters hope.

Jacob's first three sons had all committed grievous sins. However, because our good God keeps all of His promises, they receive His grace.

When you and I do not understand certain moments that happen in our lives, we can cling to God's promises—because they are good, faithful, and true. We can fully place our hope in Him because grace and forgiveness reign because of Jesus.

Our sin could have easily cost us every blessing. However, God sees us through the blood of His Son, which cleanses us white as snow.

Because of Jesus, we will never know the wrath of God or be downgraded in His affections.

Go Quiet, Go Deep

Quiet your mind from distractions and pull your Bible close. Bow your head and ask Jesus to make His Word and today's lesson personal for you.

Take your time writing out 2 Timothy 1:9.

What does it mean to you personally that God calls you to a holy life for His purposes?

I pray that the boundless love, grace, and forgiveness of Jesus would penetrate every barrier today so that He can work in you and through you.

DAY 4

PROPHETIC BLESSING OVER THE TRIBE OF JUDAH

Judah, your brothers shall praise you; your hand shall be on the neck of your enemies; your father's sons shall bow down before you. (Genesis 49:8)

Nothing makes my mom happier than having all of her chicks gathered around her. If you are a mom, perhaps you can relate. Anytime one of my sisters or I ask our mom what she wants for her birthday or any other special occasion, her answer is always to have her family around her: four daughters, six grandchildren, and four great-grandchildren, along with all of the various spouses.

Our Thanksgiving and Christmas family celebrations resemble a small village, yet none of us would trade for anything the deep, abiding love and honest friendships that our family enjoys. We know beyond all shadow of a doubt that when any one of us needs help, the family cavalry rallies at the drop of a hat. And that huge blessing is due to our parent's commitment to family.

The bonds of family were important in patriarchal societies as well. As Jacob realizes that his time on earth is coming to an end, he calls his twelve sons to gather around him to receive his blessings. We have looked at the blessing he bestowed on Reuben, Simeon, and Levi. Now we come to the most significant blessing that Jacob gives—to Judah.

JUDAH WAS NOT BLAMELESS
Read Genesis 49:8–12. What stands out to you in these verses?

First of all, Jacob's blessing for Judah is the longest and most detailed among his twelve sons. As we learned on Day 3, Jacob's blessings over

Reuben, Simeon, and Levi included curses for their sinful actions. Yet Jacob includes no curses in Judah's blessing, even though Judah had also sinned.

What did Judah orchestrate in Genesis 37:26–27?

Rather than stand up to his brothers and rescue Joseph completely, Judah became a human trafficker. Then there was the whole sordid episode between Judah and his daughter-in-law, Tamar, in Genesis 38, where Judah unknowingly slept with Tamar, who conceived children as a result.

Judah's sins were much more serious than getting caught with his hand in the cookie jar. So why did Judah receive the blessing of leadership from his father instead of Reuben?

The Ruler from Judah's Lineage

This is where we take a moment to look deeper at the context and eventual recipients of Jacob's blessings. As with all of his twelve sons, the blessings Jacob spoke over each were not experienced directly by his sons but rather by the tribes that bore their names.

In Judah's blessing, Jacob prophesies about the future age of the kingdom of God through the tribe of Judah. As a whole, both Christian and Jewish scholars traditionally interpret Judah's blessing to be a prophesy of the coming Messiah—particularly verse 10.

What does Genesis 49:10 tell us?

The scepter is a symbol of royal authority. Keeping in mind that Jacob's blessing to Judah would be experienced by his tribe, the scepter and royal staff point to the fact that there will always be a ruler from Judah's lineage: our Lord Jesus Christ. *The Lutheran Study Bible* explains it this way:

> Because this is a prophecy of what will happen with Judahs descendants, we must think of the Coming One as being from the

lineage of Judah. At the same time, it says that He "comes," as if from elsewhere. The prophet Micah spoke of Him more clearly as He who would be both from Judah and at the same time from the beginning, from eternal days (Mi 5:2).[17]

Even though Jesus' earthly lineage came through the tribe of Judah, He is eternal. As the Second Person of the Trinity, Jesus first had to descend from His heavenly home to be born of a virgin and live the sinless life that we could not. And God chose the line of Judah through which to accomplish His rescue mission of love for all of mankind.

BOTH WAR AND PEACE

Another significant aspect of Jacob's blessing to Judah is the fact that it contains contrasting elements of war and peace.

In Genesis 49:8–10a, Jacob prophesies that Judah's offspring will be a victor with His hand on the enemy's neck, a crouching lion, and a scepter-holding ruler.

In Genesis 49:10b–12, Jacob prophesies that Judah's offspring will one day live in peace when the coming kingdom of God will be ruled by the Prince of Peace. As a result of this blessing, you and I can live in the peace of God today. How do you see that truth in the following verses?

Philippians 4:7

John 14:27

God does not keep secret from us that we find peace and contentment in Christ alone. From Scripture, we know that His peace is ours but living and abiding in His peace is the key. That is simple to say, but not so simple to live out.

How have you experienced the peace of God? If so, what did that look and feel like?

Regardless of the war over our souls that rages around us and in the heavenly realms each day, Jesus is our Prince of Peace. Looking to Jesus' cross and empty tomb, and knowing He sits at the right hand of the Father, enables us to live and experience His peace even amid the chaos.

THE LION OF JUDAH

As we have already learned, through Jacob's blessing over Judah and through Judah's lineage, Jesus is our Lion of Judah. That sounds mighty and grand, but how does that translate into our daily lives according to the following verses?

Revelation 1:8

Revelation 22:13

Hebrews 12:2

John 6:35

1 Thessalonians 1:10

John 10:11

And those are just the tip of the iceberg! He is also these:

- Our "great high priest" (Hebrews 4:14)
- Lord over all (Philippians 2:9–11)
- The "light of the world" (John 8:12)
- The "Lamb of God" (John 1:29)
- Our Redeemer (Job 19:25)
- Our Rock (1 Corinthians 10:4)

The list goes on and on. Through the tribe of Judah, God ordained that you and I would be gifted with a Savior who would save us from sin and death so that we could live and reign with Him throughout eternity.

Jesus is our Door, the Way, the Truth, the Life, and our Victorious One. He is our Wonderful Counselor, Mighty God, Everlasting Father, and Prince of Peace.

Like Judah, we are undeserving of such grace from our Father. Yet God chose Judah's tribe by grace alone to bring us the Messiah. Unlike Judah, you and I can experience the blessing of that holy inheritance today.

No matter what we face throughout our lifetime, one day, we will see Him face-to-face. Nothing can separate us from His love. And He will wipe away every tear and usher us into His glorious presence for all eternity.

What an unimaginable, glorious, magnificent day that will be!

Go Quiet, Go Deep

Quiet your mind from distractions and pull your Bible close. Bow your head and ask Jesus to make His Word and today's lesson personal for you.

Take your time writing out Romans 8:38–39.

What does it mean to you personally that nothing can separate you from God's love?

I pray that the boundless love, grace, and forgiveness of Jesus penetrate would every barrier today so that He can work in you and through you.

DAY 5

PROPHETIC BLESSINGS
FOR JACOB'S REMAINING SONS

Joseph is a fruitful bough, a fruitful bough by a spring; his branches run over the wall. The archers bitterly attacked him, shot at him, and harassed him severely, yet his bow remained unmoved; his arms were made agile by the hands of the Mighty One of Jacob. (Genesis 49:22–24)

Before writing this study, I had never undertaken an in-depth journey to learn in greater detail both the meaning and results of Jacob's blessings over his twelve sons. Today, we will look at how Jacob blessed his eight remaining sons and what we can learn from each.

Rather than read today's text in one large chunk, we will read each section as Jacob's blessing applied to each son. This will enable us to go a bit deeper and lend greater understanding to each blessing.

Since their names were later used to identify Israel's twelve tribes, the meaning behind the names of Jacob's sons is significant as well. Also, the nonchronological order in which Jacob blessed his twelve sons in Genesis 49 is very interesting—as is the assignment of symbolism to each blessing in the text.

JACOB'S BLESSING FOR ZEBULUN
Read Genesis 49:13.

Jacob's fifth blessing skips to his tenth-born son, Zebulun, who was the brother right ahead of Joseph. The name *Zebulun* means "abode," and the symbol Jacob relates to his blessing is a ship.

What does 1 Chronicles 12:33 tell us about the tribe of Zebulun?

Here we see the tribe of Zebulun supplying David's army with the largest number of warriors of any tribe, which set Zebulun's tribe apart for their faithfulness. Archaeologists believe that this tribe probably settled on land situated between the Sea of Galilee and the Mediterranean Sea. Hence, the symbol of the ship for Zebulun's tribe.

JACOB'S BLESSING FOR ISSACHAR
Read Genesis 49:14–15.

Jacob's sixth blessing is given to his ninth-born son, Issachar. The name *Issachar* means "reward," and the symbol of his blessing is a donkey.

In Numbers 26:25, how large was the tribe of Issachar?

Issachar's tribe was the third largest of Israel's twelve tribes. However, due to foreign enemies taking advantage of their sheer size (among other factors), they became a people pulled back into the bondage of slavery.

JACOB'S BLESSING FOR DAN
Read Genesis 49:16–18.

Jacob's seventh blessing skips back up to his fifth-born son, Dan. The name *Dan* means "judgment," and the symbol of his blessing is a serpent. As verse 16 states plainly, Dan was a tribe of judges.

Who was one of Dan's judges according to Judges 13:2–3, 24?

Even though Samson was one of Dan's most prominent judges, he often disobeyed the Lord by letting his anger and lust get the best of him. This resulted in his death at the hands of the Philistines, even as he brought down their house on all their heads by collapsing its support pillars (Judges 16:28–31).

Scripture reveals that the tribe of Dan was responsible for introducing idolatry into Israel (Judges 18:30) and, to God's great sorrow, became a center for idol worship in Israel (Amos 8:14). Some scholars believe that Dan's symbol of the serpent refers to the notion of the Antichrist found in some Christian traditions.

The tribe of Dan is not listed among the 144,000 in Revelation 7:5–8. However, Ezekiel 48 lists the tribe of Dan first on God's heavenly roll call. And we can take heart as we see here again God's grace and redemption regardless of our sin.

Jacob's Blessing for Gad
Read Genesis 49:19.

Jacob's eighth blessing moves up the line to his seventh-born son, Gad. The name of *Gad* means "good fortune," and the symbol of his blessing is a raider.

What did the tribe of Gad do according to 1 Chronicles 12:8?

Gad sent mighty warriors to David during a time when Israel desperately needed them. And even though the tribe of Gad was oppressed for a time (Jeremiah 49:1), Gad rose triumphantly.

This provides such a wonderful word of hope for you and me! When we are engaged in severe spiritual battles and think we may lose the fight, we will always emerge victorious because Jesus, our Victor, already won the war against our deadly enemies.

Jacob's Blessing for Asher
Read Genesis 49:20.

Jacob's ninth blessing also moves up the line to his eighth-born son, Asher. The name *Asher* means "happy," and the symbol of his blessing is rich food. Based on those two facts alone, I want to be part of the tribe of Asher. Can I get an amen?

How does Moses describe the tribe of Asher in Deuteronomy 33:24?

Between the reference to dipping their foot in oil and enjoying royal dainties, the land where Asher's tribe settled likely contained luxuries in addition to people's daily necessities. What a beautiful picture of how Jesus does immeasurably more than we can ever ask or imagine (Ephesians 3:20). Happy feet!

JACOB'S BLESSING FOR NAPHTALI
Read Genesis 49:21.

Jacob's tenth blessing is given to his sixth-born son, Naphtali. The name *Naphtali* means "wrestle," and the symbol of his blessing is a doe. In the New King James Version, Genesis 49:21 is translated, "Naphtali is a deer let loose; He uses beautiful words."

What does Matthew 4:12–16 tell us about Naphtali?

Jesus did much of His ministry around the region of Naphtali. As Jesus' words brought people (including you and me) out of the darkness and into His glorious light, Naphtali's description of "beautiful words" is most certainly true.

JACOB'S BLESSING FOR JOSEPH
Read Genesis 49:22–26.

Now we come to longest blessing that Jacob gives: this one to his favorite son, Joseph. Jacob's eleventh blessing is given to his eleventh-born son, Joseph. The name *Joseph* means "may he add." The symbol of his blessing is fruitfulness.

Even though the archers (mainly in the form of his brothers) aimed at and attacked Joseph through hatred and deplorable betrayal, God provided protection through Joseph's deep faith and relationship with God.

Because of that deep, abiding faith to walk in God's ways, God gave Joseph more abundantly than his brothers through material blessings, including agriculture and a large family. When you and I faithfully walk with the Lord and rely on His strength, the spiritual blessings that God promises to pour over our lives will be far more than we can count.

JACOB'S BLESSING FOR BENJAMIN
Read Genesis 49:27.

Jacob's twelfth and final blessing is given to his youngest son, Benjamin. The name *Benjamin* means "son of the right hand," and the symbol of his blessing is a wolf. In fact, the text says he was a "ravenous wolf." Men from the tribe of Benjamin carried a reputation for being particularly fierce. They include:

- Saul, also called Paul (Acts 8:1–3)
- Ehud (Judges 3:15–23)
- King Saul (1 Samuel 9:1, 14:47–52)

Although these men were fierce in battle, notice that Paul was also fierce about sharing the Gospel message of Jesus.

What did Paul endure for the sake of the Gospel according to 2 Corinthians 11:16–33?

May you and I be half as fierce in our commitment and zeal to share the Gospel message of Jesus Christ as Paul from the tribe of Benjamin.

HELPFUL CHART OF BIRTH AND BLESSING ORDER

To recap what we studied above, on the following page is a chart to mark and keep handy for future reference. Although not previously mentioned, you can see here the meaning of the names Reuben, Simeon, and Levi and the symbols of their blessings.

Son (by birth order)	Meaning of name	Order of blessing	Symbol of blessing[18]
1. Reuben	Behold, a son	1	Reckless
2. Simeon	Hearing	2	Violence
3. Levi	Attachment	3	Violence
4. Judah	Praise	4	Lion
5. Dan	Judgment	7	Serpent
6. Naphtali	Wrestle	10	Doe
7. Gad	Good fortune	8	Raider
8. Asher	Happy	9	Rich food
9. Issachar	Reward	6	Donkey
10. Zebulun	Abode	5	Ships
11. Joseph	May he add	11	Fruitful
12. Benjamin	Son of the right hand	12	Wolf

Jacob's blessings were prophetic over his sons' lives, as well as those of his two grandsons Manasseh and Ephraim. God's blessings over you and me as His children are just as personal, powerful, and prophetic.

In Christ, we have received "every spiritual blessing in the heavenly places" (Ephesians 1:3). As we submit to His leading and guidance throughout our lives, redemption is ours because Jesus is our very great reward.

Go Quiet, Go Deep

Quiet your mind from distractions and pull your Bible close. Bow your head and ask Jesus to make His Word and today's lesson personal for you.

Take your time writing out Genesis 15:1.

What does it mean to you personally that Jesus (and His boundless grace) is our very great reward?

I pray that the boundless love, grace, and forgiveness of Jesus would penetrate every barrier today so that He can work in you and through you.

WEEK 8

GOD MEANT IT FOR GOOD

Genesis 49:28–50:26

"God meant it for good." When the life we hoped for takes a nosedive, those words convey a deep, abiding trust in the Lord. In those moments, the easy path is to whine, complain, and blame. But acknowledging that God knew best all along—and will faithfully continue working in our best interest according to His will—comes from a heart completely transformed by Him. None of us come to love or forgive naturally. It is the Holy Spirit who enables us to even think toward either.

When Joseph uttered these words to his brothers, he did not stand to gain or profit from them. He was the Old Testament poster child for how God can bring beauty from ashes. In speaking such grace-filled words, Joseph seeks to mend emotional and relational fences that had been broken through no fault of his own.

To acknowledge that God meant our pain for good is the mark of a mature, spiritually wise follower of Jesus. It reflects an attitude of building bridges instead of grabbing explosives. God means our pain for good. And we can be content with the word *good* because what God calls good is good enough.

DAY 1 The Death of Jacob (*Genesis 49:28–33*)

DAY 2 Allowing Time to Mourn (*Genesis 50:1–3*)

DAY 3 Honoring a Patriarch (*Genesis 50:4–14*)

DAY 4 God Meant It for Good (*Genesis 50:15–21*)

DAY 5 The Death of Joseph (*Genesis 50:22–26*)

KEY QUESTIONS:

- If you have lost a parent, how has it reshaped your family dynamic?

- Because the Holy Spirit's work enables you to love and forgive, how can you take the step toward extending forgiveness to someone who has hurt you?

- When the Lord calls you home, what will people say about you and your faith?

THE DEATH OF JACOB

When Jacob finished commanding his sons, he drew up his feet into the bed and breathed his last and was gathered to his people. (Genesis 49:33)

Deadlines are both intimidating and necessary. As a writer, I thank the sweet Lord above for deadlines. That may seem odd unless you can identify with being a certified, completely geeky lifelong learner. No, that's not an official degree. Simply put, I can read *ad nauseum* about many topics of interest—*especially* biblical history, biblical cultures, and well-written commentaries.

By the time I sit down to write a book, a devotion, or even a blog post, there is often an overload of information ricocheting in my brain. The content is far too much to be contained in a book, but not enough to qualify as a commentary.

But the point is, I am thankful for deadlines. I have an adrenaline rush accompanied by a clarity of purpose when pushing toward a deadline. And when that deadline is successfully met, God provides a sense of accomplishment and celebration at seeing what He brought about.

We all have a deadline when it comes to our time on earth. Preordained by God, that is the moment when we will exhale our last breath. For a believer in Jesus, that will be an extraordinary moment as He finally welcomes us to our heavenly home. However, that moment brings sadness and grief for loved ones still here.

That is where we find ourselves in Joseph's narrative. In this bittersweet moment, God finally gathers Jacob, at 147 years old, to his eternal home.

BLESSINGS REMEMBERED
Read Genesis 49:28–33.

The scene opens with a reminder that Jacob has blessed the future twelve tribes of Israel. And as we have already studied, even though Joseph received a double portion of Jacob's blessing, the greatest gift to God's people (as is still true today) was Judah's scepter. Through Judah's line came the long-awaited Messiah and Savior of the world.

What is Jacob's final request in Genesis 49:29–30?

Even though Jacob has already made this request, he wants to ensure that his bones will rest in God's Promised Land and not a foreign one. Jacob had sojourned many miles over many years. He wanted to rest in the cave that his grandfather purchased as the family burying place.

Have you made plans for where your bones will rest? Have you let your loved ones know?

Some people tend to avoid this topic, believing it to be macabre; yet it is a necessary task. If one thing in this life is certain, it is that one day, our life will end. We have a 100 percent mortality rate.

However, for a believer in Jesus Christ, I will say it again—our last day here is the gateway to an eternity spent worshiping our Savior. Still, many people find it difficult to discuss end of life scenarios, so let's pause.

Read 2 Corinthians 4:16–18. Take a moment to write out all the hope found in these verses.

Wasting away but renewed. Momentary affliction but eternal glory. There is truly no comparison between this life and the next. And God has given every single person a purpose in life, all the way to the end, even if they cannot actively participate in it.

TIME-STOPPING EVENTS

During the last days of my dad's life, he could not get out of bed. Yet in those moments, I saw God draw our family together around Dad's bedside. For eight days, he was never alone. Mom, my sisters, and I slept in the hospital waiting room, took turns sitting with Dad in his ICU room and greeting extended family and friends who visited, and ran back and forth to Mom and Dad's house to shower, change, and return to the hospital.

Yes, those days watching Dad decline were some of the hardest in my life. But they were also some of the most cherished. The rat race of life that kept all of us running in different directions suddenly stopped. And God provided clarity as to what was most important: being there for Dad and one another.

Have you experienced such a time-stopping event in your life? If so, what did God show you through it?

I do not know about your situation, but for my family, I truly believe God ordained that pause. Our whole world was the ICU waiting room. We did not know or care what was happening outside those walls. We shared cherished moments talking about life and faith, and time did not hurry our words or interrupt deep thoughts.

Jacob Breathes His Last
What does Genesis 49:33 tell us?

At long last, after his long service to the Lord, God gathered His saint Jacob to his heavenly rest. We can almost hear God saying, "Welcome home." When it comes to a believer's death, what do the following verses tell us?

Psalm 116:15

Ecclesiastes 3:1–2a

2 Corinthians 4:7

God's people are His precious jars of clay, living here for only a season. A blip on the timeline of eternity. The question we close with today is simply: **How will you spend the rest of your blip?**

Go Quiet, Go Deep

Quiet your mind from distractions and pull your Bible close. Bow your head and ask Jesus to make His Word and today's lesson personal for you.

Take your time writing out Psalm 23:4.

What does it mean to you personally that God is with you in your valleys?

I pray that the boundless love, grace, and forgiveness of Jesus would penetrate every barrier today so that He can work in you and through you.

DAY 2

ALLOWING TIME TO MOURN

Then Joseph fell on his father's face and wept over him and kissed him. (Genesis 50:1)

Not one empty space was left on any pew. People stood lining the walls. Not one eye remained dry in the 2,200-seat church. As Mildred's casket was rolled down the center aisle, everyone stood. Out of anyone I have known up to this point in my life, Mildred truly exuded the joy of the Lord.

At age 80, Mildred Lieder (alongside her husband, Lawrence) had four children, eleven grandchildren, eighteen great-grandchildren, and numerous nieces, nephews, and friends. She taught them all through her words and actions how to love and serve Jesus well. But that was only part of her faith-filled legacy.

When Mildred became involved in a cause, she was all in—or she was not in at all. At Salem Lutheran Church, whether it was singing in the choir, serving as president of the Lutheran Women in Mission group, being a church greeter, or supporting mission endeavors to Honduras and Kenya, Mildred was all in.

In the greater Tomball community, whether it was supporting and cheering on a girl's center, school boards, a university system, the local volunteer fire department, or various other causes, Mildred was all in. And through it all, she served alongside her husband in their successful family business.

And if Mildred loved you, it was like drinking from Niagara Falls. She hugged the stuffing out of you, listened, encouraged, championed, and held nothing back. Her smile lit up every room, and if you did not already know Jesus, you would by the end of your first conversation with her. Mildred was all in.

On the day of her funeral day in April 2012, our church overflowed with flowers, tears, and people grateful to have been touched by a life well-lived. Countless stories were shared about her dedicated service and love for the Lord.

When you asked Mildred how she was doing, she always replied, "I'm blessed and highly favored by the Lord!" And if you commented on her generosity, she always replied, "You can't out-give God!" She left an incredible legacy of faith in her wake.

As today's lesson opens at Jacob's funeral, we see the huge outpouring of love and honor for this beloved patriarch. By the grace of God, Jacob left an incredible legacy of faith in his wake.

JOSEPH FELL ON HIS FATHER'S FACE
Read Genesis 50:1–3. What stands out to you in these verses?

Jacob experiences firsthand the very moment that his father passes into eternity. *And he wept.* For loved ones still on earth, weeping is a natural reaction. And this particular phrase is used a total of nine times in all of the Book of Genesis. Eight of those nine times happen in the narratives of Jacob and Joseph—two of them involving Jacob and six involving Joseph. What is happening in each instance?

Genesis 27:38

Genesis 29:11

Genesis 42:24

Genesis 43:30

Genesis 45:14

Genesis 45:15

Genesis 46:29

Genesis 50:1

Whether it was weeping in private or weeping upon someone, there were many occasions for weeping in Joseph's life. And our study up to this point certainly shows why.

What is so poignant is that every time Joseph wept *upon* someone, it was his family. After the terrible things that Joseph's brothers had done to him, sharing such an intimate moment of grief provides a beautiful display of God's redemptive power in all of their lives.

Have you ever fallen into someone's arms and wept? Who was that person, and what was the occasion?

Those are intensely private, personal moments. But when we grieve, God promises to comfort us even if no one else is around. I realize that death and grief are difficult topics to talk about. It is hard to experience either. So let's pause for a moment. Take time to write out the following verses:

Matthew 5:4

Psalm 34:18

We do not usually trust random people to hold us up when grief cripples us. Because of His great love for us, God never leaves us alone in our grief. He sends His Comforter, the Holy Spirit, to comfort us from the inside out.

JOSEPH KISSED JACOB

There are not many people who are comfortable kissing corpses. Most people instinctively recoil because there is just something unnatural about a lifeless body. When a person's life leaves his or her body, the change is instantaneous. It is strange and often frightening.

Have you ever experienced a similar situation or been in the room when a person has transitioned from this life to the next? How did you react?

Genesis 50:1 is very personal for me. Like Joseph, I did not expect to be in the room when my dad died. As my mom and I stood there sobbing on either side of him, holding his hands, I did the only thing that seemed natural: I leaned over and kissed my dad on the forehead.

It was the same way he had greeted me as an adult and the same way he made me feel better if I was sick as a child. He would kiss me on my forehead. And that gesture always made me feel loved, welcomed, and at home. So returning that gesture when Dad died was my way of telling him how much I loved him as Jesus welcomed him home in heaven.

We do not know how we will react to situations that shake the foundations of our lives until we get there. In that moment, Joseph kissed his father's forehead.

EMBALMING JACOB

Read Genesis 50:2–3.

As God's image-bearers, Jewish tradition strictly prohibits embalming a body since it is viewed as a desecration of the image of God.[19] However, Joseph orders Egypt's physicians to embalm Jacob. His brothers are silent about the matter, so the procedure goes forward.

Some scholars view Joseph's decision as proof that Joseph has abandoned his faith and embraced foreign cultural practices. However, other scholars view it as simply going along with the cultural hygiene of the day.

Which scenario do you believe is true?

Whichever way you voted, one thing is clear: God does not stop Joseph from embalming Jacob nor punishes him at any point afterward. God's inaction about Jacob's embalming demonstrates that Joseph's decision was acceptable to God. Since Jacob had made Joseph promise to carry his body back to Canaan, embalming was a wise move, indeed.

EGYPT WEPT

What is the last sentence of Genesis 50:3?

Joseph was highly esteemed by Egypt. After all, he had saved the Egyptians during a devastating seven-year famine. Now the time has come for Egypt to mourn Joseph's father. The seventy-day period comprised the forty days it took for the embalming process, plus a mourning period of thirty days. Again, such an extended grieving period shows how highly they esteemed Joseph.

As we close, Jacob lived a life that was all in. Yes, he wrestled with sin, wrestled with God, and doubted along his journey of faith, but Jacob was all in. He had experienced God's prophetic dreams come to fruition and His promises fulfilled. And he taught his family to fear, serve, and honor the Lord.

When your life on earth comes to an end, what will people say about you? I pray that you loved Jesus outrageously. Served Him wholeheartedly. Told people about Him relentlessly. And exuded His joy enthusiastically.

Will people say that you were all in? There is still time.

Go Quiet, Go Deep

Quiet your mind from distractions and pull your Bible close. Bow your head and ask Jesus to make His Word and today's lesson personal for you.

Take your time writing out Psalm 73:26.

What does it mean to you personally that as you grieve over the loss of loved ones, God is the strength of your heart?

I pray that the boundless love, grace, and forgiveness of Jesus would penetrate every barrier today so that He can work in you and through you.

DAY 3

HONORING A PATRIARCH

So Joseph went up to bury his father. With him went up all the servants of Pharaoh, the elders of his household, and all the elders of the land of Egypt, as well as all the household of Joseph, his brothers, and his father's household. (Genesis 50:7–8a)

Joseph's importance in Egypt was unquestionable. He had saved them from perishing in a catastrophic seven-year famine and served Pharaoh as a capable, faithful steward for all the land of Egypt. At Pharaoh's invitation, Joseph's people moved from Canaan and settled in the fertile land of Goshen. In lush Goshen, God's people had multiplied into a great nation.

After his father's death, Joseph's first order of business is to honor Jacob's burial wishes. As Joseph prepares to return to Canaan to bury his father, we see the full pomp and circumstance of Egypt unfold.

PHARAOH'S KINDNESS

Read Genesis 50:4–6. What stands out to you in these verses?

Even after serving Pharaoh for more than two decades by this time, Joseph still showed the proper respect that was due to the ruler. Whether Joseph and Pharaoh saw eye-to-eye, or even got along, Joseph still respected the office.

In our challenging political times, we would do well to remember such respect of office regardless of who sits behind the resolute desk in the Oval Office. What do the following verses tell us?

Romans 13:1–2

1 Thessalonians 5:12–14

Kindness and common courtesy took a hit during the coronavirus pandemic. Covering our faces and being forced to remain separated for an extended time took away some of the humanity of our communities. People found it easier to say unkind things when they did not have to see on someone's face the collateral damage that words can cause. Respecting one another—as well as our leaders—honors God and one another as God's imagebearers.

Since Scripture never indicates that Joseph left his position with Pharaoh, we can safely conclude that Joseph still serves as Egypt's prime minister. As such, receiving Pharaoh's permission to be gone for an extended period would allow measures and people to be put in place to run the affairs of state during his absence. Again, this shows Joseph's excellent administrative gifts.

Elaborate Funeral Procession
Read Genesis 50:7–9. What stands out to you in these verses?

These verses encapsulate the most ornate funeral found in all of Scripture, bar none. I have attended many funerals over the years. Some were large, others were small, some had many flowers, others had few. However, I cannot say that I have ever attended an *elaborate* funeral.

In our lifetime, we have witnessed a few funerals that we could classify as elaborate. President Kennedy's funeral was elaborate, thanks to the first lady's careful attention to detail. Sir Winston Churchill's funeral was certainly elaborate, with more than one million people packing the streets of London to honor his procession. Then there was Princess Diana's funeral, where an estimated one million mourners lined the streets near Westminster Abbey. And we cannot forget the pomp, circumstance, and splendor of Queen Elizabeth II's funeral after reigning for an unprecedented seventy years.

When one of Israel's or Judah's kings was laid to rest, what phrase is most commonly used to describe that process in the following verses?

1 Kings 2:10

1 Kings 11:43

1 Kings 14:31

They all recited basically the same one-sentence phrase that they were buried with their fathers in the City of David. However, Jacob's funeral procession is the closest in Scripture that parallels a modern-day funeral of state.

But beyond all the pomp and circumstance, that journey was personal to Joseph and his brothers. Yes, Jacob was a man of great importance and was due such honor and respect. But to Joseph, that was his dad. And you only have one dad.

EGYPT MOURNED WITH JOSEPH'S FAMILY
Read Genesis 50:10–11. What stands out to you in these verses?

Today, funerals usually have two parts: the church (or funeral home) service and the graveside burial. We cannot overlook the fact that Egypt's entire caravan made the long journey *all the way to Canaan* to attend Jacob's graveside service. Personal sacrifices of time, expense, and absence from home were necessary for each person to accompany Jacob's body to Canaan.

What does it mean to you to mourn with those who mourn? What has that looked like in your life for a grieving family member or friend?

There is one important element missing as the funeral caravan processed: Egypt's loathing toward the Hebrews. We have learned in this study that the Egyptians did not eat with Hebrews because it was an abomination to them. Such division is absent here.

Taking the time to get to know one another and work toward a common goal often erases prejudices and divisive idiosyncrasies. Just look at Jesus' disciples. How many rabbis had both zealots and tax collectors among their followers?

What does Galatians 3:28 tell us?

We are all one in Christ Jesus. Period. The ground at the foot of the cross does not have a VIP section. We are all for one, because that One is all for us.

Keeping His Promise
Read Genesis 50:12–14.

Joseph kept his promise. He could have said he was too busy at work. He could have said the journey to Canaan and back would take too much time and expense. But Joseph kept his promise, and everyone knew it.

What promise are we given in Romans 10:13?

When God makes a promise, He fulfills it because His promises ultimately lead us to His main objectives: our redemption and life everlasting with Him. In Jesus, God kept His promise and we, the redeemed, have the privilege of letting everyone know it.

Go Quiet, Go Deep

Quiet your mind from distractions and pull your Bible close. Bow your head and ask Jesus to make His Word and today's lesson personal for you.

Take your time writing out 2 Timothy 2:13.

What does it mean to you personally that even if you are not faithful to God, He remains faithful to you?

I pray that the boundless love, grace, and forgiveness of Jesus would penetrate every barrier today so that He can work in you and through you.

DAY 4

GOD MEANT IT FOR GOOD

But Joseph said to them, "Do not fear, for am I in the place of God? As for you, you meant evil against me, but God meant it for good, to bring it about that many people should be kept alive, as they are today." (Genesis 50:19–20)

The narrative of Joseph's life reads better than the best script of an Oscar-winning movie. His journey contains family strife, betrayal, attempted murder, human trafficking, sexual temptation, incarceration, liberation, concealed identity, and dramatic reconciliation. He rises in power, earns riches and wealth, and is now perfectly poised to exact revenge on the men who stole his life and dreams.

With all due respect to Hollywood, God is a much better scriptwriter. Yes, all of the drama and intrigue exists by God's design. Yet when Joseph has the world at his feet with the power to destroy those who tried to destroy him, he forgives instead of retaliates.

Through faith forged in the fire of suffering, Joseph's example of forgiveness showcases the heart of the Gospel: love.

LINGERING GUILT

Read Genesis 50:15. What stands out to you in this verse?

In modern-day terminology, Joseph's brothers are expecting a *Godfather*-type movie scenario. The head of the family is gone, so now the time has come for Joseph to settle old scores by sending out his goons. *Wrong.* The world operates on revenge, but God operates on grace.

Have you ever experienced lingering doubt about a past sin? If so, what happened?

Has God enabled you to release that lingering guilt to Him? If so, how has that been a blessing?

If not, what is preventing you from releasing that guilt to God?

One of the most harmful myths floating around our culture goes like this: "God has forgiven you; now you just need to forgive yourself." It may sound like great advice, but it's a waterless pit. The last place we should look for healing is from within ourselves. This mindset assumes that God has forgiven you 80 percent of the way, and you need to muster up the remaining 20 percent.

Let me put it another way. "Forgive yourself" is the equivalent of shouting at a dying person, "Heal yourself!" The broken, sinful person staring at you in the mirror has no power to heal the broken, sinful person staring back. True healing can come only from God.

What does John 8:36 tell us?

Only the Son can truly set us free from lingering guilt over past sin. We cannot forgive ourselves—that's God's job. Joseph's brothers could not forgive themselves either, but instead of looking up, they looked around.

Old Habits Die Hard
Read Genesis 50:16–21.

Did you notice how old habits die hard? Deceit and lies landed Joseph's brothers in trouble in the first place. So once again they backslide into their old habits and come up with a plan among themselves.

What is their plan, according to the verses above?

First of all, the brothers are too afraid to even appear before Joseph, so they send a message instead. That would be like texting the president of the United States with a message like this: "Our mom said to forgive me for breaking your bicycle and not to hurt me back because I know I was wrong. She said you should forgive me." If Jacob said that, it happened offstage because Scripture does not mention such a message from Jacob.

What is Joseph's response in Genesis 50:17?

Perhaps Joseph wept because the brothers were still holding onto the suspicion of retaliation for decades. Perhaps he wept because he perceived respect and remorse in their message. In either case, Joseph wept.

God Meant It for Good

After sending the message, the brothers show up before Joseph and again bow down before him. As an aside, Joseph was blessed to see his original prophetic dreams come true each time his brothers bowed down to him.

And what is Joseph's response to their fear-filled request in Genesis 50:19–20?

God meant it for good. Those words come from a man greatly used by God, a man who learned strength in adversity and forgiveness despite hurt. One of the hardest lessons we learn as Christians is how to love one another as Christ loves us.

As you look back on your life, do you cherish your suffering or your blessings the most?

Although blessings from God are a beautiful gift, I find that I cherish the suffering more. The lessons God taught me in the fire of suffering could not have been learned any other way. Abundant, fruitful ministry has come more often from those suffering places.

God gives us the courage to stand when adversity strikes, confident that we are never alone in our suffering because Christ is with us and sends His Holy Spirit as our Comforter.

Nowhere in Joseph's narrative do we ever see him reminding his brothers of what they did to him. We do not see Joseph holding it over their heads. We do not see Joseph withholding love or necessities from his brothers. By the grace of God, Joseph had completely forgiven his brothers for the wrongs they committed against him.

As Joseph has done from the time that he revealed his identity to now, he again must reassure his brothers to rid them of fear and get them to trust him. He faithfully directs their gaze up to God—the only source that will give them the peace that passes all understanding.

In Joseph's love for his brothers, we hear the same grace of God that you and I receive when we fear His retaliation instead of His redemption.

Jesus faithfully reassures us over and again. Get rid of fear. Look up. Trust Him.

Go Quiet, Go Deep

Quiet your mind from distractions and pull your Bible close. Bow your head and ask Jesus to make His Word and today's lesson personal for you.

Take your time writing out John 14:1.

What does it mean to you personally that God does not want your heart troubled by lingering guilt over past sin?

I pray that the boundless love, grace, and forgiveness of Jesus would penetrate every barrier today so that He can work in you and through you.

DAY 5

THE DEATH OF JOSEPH

So Joseph died, being 110 years old. They embalmed him, and he was put
in a coffin in Egypt. (Genesis 50:26)

The first time I drafted my Last Will and Testament, it was a sobering
process. Not so much that I would die one day, but who would inherit
what after I was gone.

I gave much thought to my possessions—who had special connections
to various items, and who needed my home and car the most. As I was telling a Christian sister about my difficulty, she asked if I had included a Christian Preamble in my will. I did not even know such a thing was a thing.

Thinking such an inclusion would be complicated, and really not even
knowing what it was, I started researching. But the definition was simple—a
Christian Preamble is a way to begin your will with a straightforward statement of faith. It would serve as my final way to witness the love and grace of
Jesus to family and friends.

I had been so focused on my stuff that I forgot to focus on my Savior.

Joseph did not have such an issue.

JOSEPH'S TIME
Read Genesis 50:22–26. What stands out to you in these verses?

At 110 years old, Joseph's time on earth comes to a close. Joseph spent
his entire adulthood—ninety-three years—in Egypt. And for Egyptians, in a
time when average life expectancy was between forty and fifty years, the age
of 110 was significant and considered to be a divine blessing.

What we have discovered is that Joseph's commitment and trust in God
was the true divine blessing. As Joseph prepares to join in heaven the patriarchs who preceded him, it is important to remember that God's initial

covenant with his grandfather Abraham happened two hundred years before. Yet when Joseph died, not one descendant of Abraham even lived in
the Promised Land. Including Joseph. Nevertheless, Joseph's trust in God
never wavered.

DYING WELL

As Joseph approaches the end of his life, he is ready. He has seen his
children grow and welcome children of their own. Yet another sign of God's
faithfulness as His people continue to be fruitful and multiply.

By all accounts, Joseph had lived a life that honored God, and he wanted
his death to do likewise. Often, the words of faith-filled believers who have
undergone severe trials in their lives provide encouragement to those of us
still fighting the good fight.

For instance, right before French theologian, pastor, and reformer John
Calvin died, he dictated a letter to a friend, which said this:

> I have great difficulty in breathing and expect at any time to
> breathe my last. It is enough for me to live and die in Christ,
> who is gain to those who belong to him, whether in life or in
> death.[20]

When we look through Scripture, we are given beautiful examples
through the apostle Paul of what it means for a believer in Jesus to die well.
How do you see that in the following passages?

Philippians 1:20

2 Timothy 4:7

However, the best example ever given to us in all of Scripture on how to
die well came from the lips of Jesus.

Write out Luke 23:46.

Have you given any thought to dying well? If so, what does that entail?

What is universally true about dying well is that you must live and die by trusting God. Because, like Joseph, trusting God encompasses both good times and difficult times. Whether in Potiphar's prison or Pharaoh's private chamber, Joseph trusted God.

JOSEPH STILL LOOKS FORWARD
What does Joseph say to his brothers in Genesis 50:24?

Joseph could have spent his last days looking back at how his life might have been. At the loss of his beloved father. At the two-decade estrangement between himself and his brothers. Instead, Joseph chooses to look forward. He tells his brothers that God *will* visit them. That God *will* rescue them from Egypt. What a beautiful witness to his family.

Among others, the apostle Paul also focused on looking forward.

What does Philippians 3:13–14 tell us?

Yes, you and I will likely experience touches of nostalgia, but for the most part, as people of hope and grafted recipients of God's promises, we joyfully look forward and not back.

Like his father before him (and carried out by Joseph's command [see Genesis 50:2–3]), Joseph chooses to be embalmed before burial and instructs his brothers accordingly. As Egypt's prime minister, Joseph would be buried in Egypt; however, Joseph knew his final resting place was in the Promised Land.

CLOSING

As a follower of Christ, you will one day be ushered into His glorious presence. In the last several weeks walking through the life of Joseph, we have seen time and again how a deep, abiding faith in God's promises makes all the difference.

The greatest legacy Joseph left was a legacy of faith, not possessions and power. Whether in a waterless pit, unjust prison, or Pharaoh's banquet room, Joseph kept his eyes on God and His sacred purposes.

May you and I live and die as well as Joseph did.

Go Quiet, Go Deep

Quiet your mind from distractions and pull your Bible close. Bow your head and ask Jesus to make His Word and today's lesson personal for you.

Take your time writing out Philippians 1:21.

What does it mean to you personally that to live is Christ and to die is gain?

I pray that the boundless love, grace, and forgiveness of Jesus would penetrate every barrier today so that He can work in you and through you.

EPILOGUE

It would have been easy for Joseph to become bitter and angry. His brothers had betrayed him, sold him into slavery, and stolen the life he had planned.

Perhaps your situation is not too far removed from Joseph's. Maybe you struggle with bitterness or anger from people or circumstances derailing the life you had planned.

Yet when God turns your heart toward Him in faith and you entrust your life and future into His loving care, His plans will bring a sense of awe and gratitude at what He accomplished.

You and I often choose life paths that are comfortable and will bring pleasure. And even though God loves you more than you can fathom, He is far more concerned about your character than your comfort, your purpose than your pleasure.

Jesus told His disciples: *"In the world you will have tribulation. But take heart; I have overcome the world"* (John 16:33). Jesus says those very words to you, His modern-day disciple.

Joseph faced many unexpected challenges as he followed God's plan for his life. Yet at each step of the way, Scripture revealed that God was with him. *God never left Joseph's side.* And the same is true for you and me.

God also blessed Joseph with times of joy and plenty. Joseph enjoyed the best that Egypt had to offer and was blessed with a wife and children to walk alongside him.

Joseph trusted God and extended forgiveness to his brothers. And through that process, God prevented bitterness and anger from taking hold in Joseph's heart and mind. Through trial and tribulation, God forged in Joseph the strength, resourcefulness, and tenacity to navigate nations through a deadly famine. God's plan for Joseph had a much larger purpose beyond his own circumstances.

So regardless of where life's pathways lead you, I pray that you keep looking up to the Lord. Keep trusting that He has you in His loving care. Keep extending forgiveness to those who hurt you so that anger and bitterness do not take hold. Trust that God never lets you go. Trust that His plan through you has a much larger purpose beyond your own life.

And most of all, I pray that you come to know God more deeply along your journey. His perfect, abiding love for you never wavers. And His plan for your life will turn out far greater than you ever dreamed.

REFERENCES

Cromwell, Jennifer, "Caring for Cows in Ancient Egypt," Papyrus Stories (website), May 27, 2020, https://papyrus-stories.com/2020/05/27/caring-for-cows-in-ancient-egypt/.

Guzik, David, "Forgetfulness and Fruitfulness," Enduring Word (website), accessed on July 7, 2022, https://enduringword.com/forgetfulness-and-fruitfulness/amp/.

Guzik, David, "Genesis 49—The Blessing of the Sons of Jacob," Enduring Word (website), accessed on July 31, 2022, https://enduringword.com/bible-commentary/genesis-49/.

Jones, R. David, "The Butler and the Baker," Bible Facts (website), accessed on July 16, 2022, http://www.bible-facts.info/commentaries/ot/thebutlerandthebaker.htm.

Kendall, R. T., *God Meant It for Good* (Fort Mill: MorningStar Publications, 2001).

Lessing, R. Reed, *Deliver Us: God's Rescue Story in the Book of Exodus* (St. Louis: Concordia Publishing House, 2022), 21–22.

Life Application Study Bible (Tyndale House Publishers, 2005).

Lutheran Bible Companion, Vol. 1: Introduction and Old Testament (St. Louis: Concordia Publishing House, 2014).

The Lutheran Study Bible (St. Louis: Concordia Publishing House, 2009).

Mark, Joshua J., "Canaan," World History Encyclopedia, October 23, 2018, https://www.worldhistory.org/canaan/.

National Geographic Society, "Pharaohs," National Geographic, May 20, 2022, https://education.nationalgeographic.org/resource/pharaohs.

NIV Archaeological Study Bible (Grand Rapids: Zondervan, 2005).

NIV Cultural Backgrounds Study Bible (Grand Rapids: Zondervan, 2016).

NLT Study Bible (Carol Stream: Tyndale House Publishers, 2008).

Pyle, Donna. *Forgiveness: Received from God, Extended to Others* (St. Louis: Concordia Publishing House, 2017).

Strong's Hebrew Lexicon (ESV), Blue Letter Bible (website), https://www.

blueletterbible.org/.

The Companion Bible: The Authorized Version of 1611 with Structures and Notes, Critical, Explanatory and Suggestive with 198 Appendixes (Kregel Publications, 1999).

Walton, John H., *Cultural Background Study Bible* (NKJV) (New York: Harper Collins Publishers, 2019).

Walton, John H., *The IVP Bible Background Commentary: Old Testament* (Downers Grove: InterVarsity Press, 2001).

ACKNOWLEDGMENTS

Thank you to my family and friends who prayed this book into reality. You bring such joy, encouragement, and love into my life. I love you beyond measure.

Thank you to my ministry board, who carried the ball when I was holed away writing this study. God has placed you here for such a time as this, and I am grateful beyond measure for each of you.

Most of all, thank You, Lord, for the path You chose for my life. I would never have dreamed of it, but now cannot imagine any other. You bring me to my knees, and I pray that You keep me there.

Endnotes

1 Hansen, David G., "Moses and Hatshepsut," *Bible and Spade* 16, no. 1 (Winter 2003), https://biblearchaeology.org/research /exodus-from-egypt/3090-moses-and-hatshepsut.

2 Chaignot, Mary Jane, "The Egyptian Pharaohs with Joseph," BibleWise, accessed January 7, 2022, https://www.biblewise.com /bible_study/characters/egyptian-pharaohs.php.

3 Editors of Encyclopedia Britannica, "Sesostris III, King of Egypt," Britannica, January 25, 2011, https://www.britannica.com/biography /Sesostris-III.

4 First Lutheran Cape Cod, "That Coat of Many Colors," August 12, 2020, https://firstcapecod.org/that-coat-of-many-colors/.

5 Janzen, Mark, "What We Know About Slavery in Egypt," TheTorah. com, 2016, http://www.thetorah.com/article/what-we-know-about -slavery-in-egypt.

6 *The Lutheran Study Bible* (St. Louis: Concordia Publishing House, 2009), 77–78.

7 Kyle, M. G., "Heliopolis (On)," Bible Hub, accessed on July 19, 2022, https://bibleatlas.org/heliopolis.htm.

8 Henry, Matthew, *Commentary on Genesis 41*, Blue Letter Bible (website), accessed on July 19, 2022, https://www.blueletterbible.org /Comm/mhc/Gen/Gen_041.cfm?a=41001.

9 *The Lutheran Study Bible* (St. Louis: Concordia Publishing House, 2009), 2123, fn 11:14.

10 Kendall, R. T., *God's Servant or His Friend?* R.T. Kendall Ministries, accessed on July 20, 2022, https://rtkendallministries.com /gods-servant-or-his-friend#:~:text=Martin%20Luther%20said %20you%20must%20know%20God%20as,friends.%20The %20Eleven%20had%20been%20servants%20of%20Jesus.

11 Tests are quoted from Pyle, Donna. *Forgiveness: Received from God, Extended to Others* (St. Louis: Concordia Publishing House, 2017), 71.

12 *The Lutheran Study Bible* (St. Louis: Concordia Publishing House, 2009), 85, fn 44:34.

13 Assmann, J. and Zev Farber, TheTorah.com, "Shepherds and Eating with Hebrews: An Abomination to the Egyptians?," https://thetorah.com/article/shepherds-and-eating-with-hebrews-an-abomination-to-the-egyptians.

14 The National WWII Museum, "Rationing," accessed July 28, 2022, https://www.nationalww2museum.org/war/articles/rationing#:~:text=The%20government%20began%20rationing%20certain,canned%20milk%20the%20following%20March.

15 Reid, Kathryn, "1980s Ethiopia famine: Facts, FAQs, and how to help," World Vision, accessed July 28, 2022, https://www.worldvision.org/disaster-relief-news-stories/1980s-ethiopia-famine-facts.

16 *The Lutheran Study Bible* (St. Louis: Concordia Publishing House, 2009), 88, fn 47:14.

17 *The Lutheran Study Bible* (St. Louis: Concordia Publishing House, 2009), 91, fn 49:10.

18 *NIV Cultural Backgrounds Study Bible* (Zondervan, 2016), p. 81.

19 Lamm, Maurice, "Autopsy and Embalming of a Jewish Body," Chabad.org, accessed on August 1, 2022, https://www.chabad.org/library/article_cdo/aid/281548/jewish/Autopsy-and-Embalming-of-a-Jewish-Body.htm.

20 Beza, Theodore, *The Life of John Calvin* (Evangelical Press), 116, 118.